TEN DAYS
TO A
SUCCESSFUL
MEMORY

Revised Edition

TEN DAYS TO A SUCCESSFUL MEMORY

Revised Edition

Dr. Joyce Brothers
Edward P. F. Eagan

A SPECTRUM BOOK

Prentice-Hall, Inc., Englewood Cliffs, New Jersey 07632

Library of Congress Cataloging in Publication Data

Brothers, Joyce.
   Ten days to a successful memory.

     Rev. ed. of: 10 days to a successful memory. 1957.
    "A Spectrum Book."
    Includes index.
     1. Mnemonics.   2. Memory.   I. Eagan, Edward P. F.
(Patrick Francis) (date).   II. Brothers, Joyce.
10 days to a successful memory.   III. Title.   IV. Title:
10 days to a successful memory.
BF385.B788 1984   153.1'2   84-8207
ISBN 0-13-903600-8
ISBN 0-13-903592-3 (pbk.)

This book is available at a special discount when ordered in bulk quantities. Contact Prentice-Hall, Inc., General Publishing Division, Special Sales, Englewood Cliffs, N.J. 07632.

© 1984 by Prentice-Hall, Inc., Englewood Cliffs, New Jersey 07632
A SPECTRUM BOOK

ISBN 0-13-903600-8

ISBN 0-13-903592-3 {PBK.}

10 9 8 7 6 5 4 3 2

Printed in the United States of America

Editorial/production supervision: Joe O'Donnell Jr.
Cover design: Hal Siegel
Cover illustration: Ken Joudrey
Manufacturing buyer: Edward J. Ellis

Prentice-Hall International, Inc., *London*
Prentice-Hall of Australia Pty. Limited, *Sydney*
Prentice-Hall Canada Inc., *Toronto*
Prentice-Hall of India Private Limited, *New Delhi*
Prentice-Hall of Japan, Inc., *Tokyo*
Prentice-Hall of Southeast Asia Pte. Ltd., *Singapore*
Whitehall Books Limited, *Wellington, New Zealand*
Editora Prentice-Hall do Brasil Ltda., *Rio de Janeiro*

To my dearest mother, Estelle, my husband, Milton, daughter, Lisa, son-in-law, Amir, and grandson, Micah, whose love and devotion I cannot forget.

Dr. Joyce Brothers, a noted psychologist, is an NBC Radio Network personality, columnist, author, business consultant, wife, and mother. A United Press International poll has named her one of the "ten most influential women" and a Gallup survey cited her as one of the "ten most admired women" in America.

Dr. Brothers is a regular columnist for *Good Housekeeping* magazine and a news commentator for NIWS syndicated television news service. Her daily column for King Features Syndicate is published in newspapers worldwide.

A graduate of Cornell University, Dr. Brothers received her Ph.D. from Columbia University. She was a member of the faculty of Hunter College and Columbia University for six years and is now a frequent lecturer at universities across the country.

Dr. Brothers currently resides in Fort Lee, New Jersey, with her internist husband, Dr. Milton Brothers, and their daughter Lisa.

CONTENTS

ACKNOWLEDGMENTS

The photograph that appears top left on page 177 and on pages 181, 187, and 190; the photograph that appears top left on page 178 and on pages 181, 187, and 192; the photograph that appears bottom right on page 178 and on pages 182 and 189; and the photograph that appears bottom left on page 179 and on pages 182, 187, and 191 are by Irene Springer.

The photograph that appears top right on page 177 and on pages 182, 187, and 192; the photograph that appears bottom right on page 177 and on pages 187 and 189; and the photograph that appears top left on page 180 and on page 191 are from Brigham Young University and by Mark A. Philbrick.

The photograph that appears top right on page 178 and on pages 181, 187, and 190; the photograph that appears bottom right on page 179 and on pages 187 and 190; and the photograph that appears top right on page 180 and on pages 187 and 191 are by Ken Karp.

The photograph that appears bottom left on page 178 and on pages 182 and 193 and the photograph that appears top left on page 179 and on pages 187 and 192 are by Mark Mangold, U.S. Census Bureau.

The photograph that appears bottom left on page 180 and on pages 187 and 193 is by Laimute E. Druskis.

The photograph that appears bottom right on page 180 and on pages 187 and 190 is courtesy of HUD.

The photograph that appears top right on page 179 and on pages 187 and 191 is courtesy of the New York Convention & Visitors Bureau.

The photograph that appears bottom left on page 176 and on pages 181 and 192 is by John Pitkin.

TEN DAYS
TO A
SUCCESSFUL
MEMORY
Revised Edition

THE JOYCE BROTHERS STORY

"Can I use my memory as effectively as you?"

I have only one answer to that question—and I have been asked it countless times since I won the top prize on The $64,000 Question television program. My answer is:

"Certainly—absolutely—without any doubt!"

Just as I was able to make use of my memory to prepare so so that I could go on a quiz program successfully, so can you use your memory for anything you want.

It doesn't mean that you necessarily are going to become a quiz-show winner. That probably is not your purpose in learning to use your memory efficiently and successfully.

It does mean, however, that you are going to be able to make the fullest use of your power to remember. And best of all, you can learn the technique of how to do this in just ten days' time.

WHY THIS BOOK WAS WRITTEN

This book was written because literally thousands of people have asked me what the secret of my "success" was. I invariably answered that there was no secret—I only made use of that wonderful little machine, the brain.

MY SECRET CAN BE YOUR SECRET _____

This, then, is the little machine that is the secret. It is my secret—and it can be your secret.

What I have been able to do because of my memory, you, too, can do. And you can do it just as easily, if you follow the plan that I have outlined in the following chapters of this book.

This is not a gimmick-game of memory. There are no lists of hundreds or thousands of association words to memorize before you can start. There is no stage trickery.

This is a practical method of increasing your power to remember—successfully. It is a tried and true method. It is the result of years and years of psychological studies into the powers of the brain.

YOU'LL SUCCEED IF YOU HAVE A REASON _____

As I explain further in the book, you must have a reason for wanting to improve your memory.

Such motivation is a vital necessity.

But I know that *you* have a reason. If you did not you would not be reading this book now.

I first had a reason to improve my memory when I was going to high school.

My parents are both professional people. They have both successfully used their education to advantage. They are both successful people in their professions.

As a schoolgirl, they insisted that I pay attention to my work in the classroom. They demanded that I do my homework thoroughly. They felt that I should always get better-than-average grades.

I, too, felt this way. But, like any young girl, I wanted to go out on dates as often as I could.

Yet, if I did not do my homework, I could not go out for the evening. If I did not keep up my grades in school, my social life would be cut down accordingly.

MAKING MY MEMORY WORK FOR ME _____

That was when I realized that I had to develop my memory so that I could learn more quickly, maintain my grades in school, and still have as much time as possible left for me to "date."

Some years later, I again had a reason to use my memory powers. This reason led me to the point where I again made use of my memory-efficiency to good advantage.

For some years after I married, I continued to work. My husband was studying medicine. I was teaching psychology at Hunter College in New York City.

Then our baby daughter was born. I took a leave of absence from my teaching post so that I could play the role of mother to my child.

This was a wonderful experience for me. We love our daughter immensely. We have a great deal of pleasure from her.

But, unfortunately, with our income reduced because I was no longer teaching, and with the growth of our family, economic pressures began to pile up. The pressure on us reached the point where it meant a major decision would have to be made.

FINDING THE ANSWER TO A PROBLEM _____

There were two answers to our problem:

1. My husband would have to interrupt his medical studies— for how long we could not guess; or,
2. I would have to leave my child in the hands of another person for a great portion of the day so that I could go back to teaching.

Neither answer was the right one for us. Neither was even remotely satisfactory in our view.

That meant only one thing—some other answer had to be found. Some other way of bringing in money had to be devised.

If we did not get money soon, it meant an unfortunate disruption in the life of our happy home.

As we sat and watched television one evening, the thought struck me:

Why not try a television quiz show?

THE COURSE OF ACTION SEEMS CLEAR _____

That seemed to be the answer! I spent a week watching all the quiz shows that were on the television channels. The biggest jackpot question program was the one I was interested in.

It paid $64,000.

What a boon to us if I could get on it and could successfully answer the list of questions that the producers would have me answer.

I spent another week studying the program's format and making my next big decision. From watching carefully, I was able to determine what categories of questions were available to the contestants who were successful in getting on this television show.

I wrote down the entire list of subjects from which I could choose if I were successful in getting on the program. From among this list I had to find something about which I had a thorough knowledge. Psychology, my profession, was not included among the suggested topics.

I then wrote down a complete list of my own particular interests—including my studies, pastimes, and hobbies.

Comparing both lists, I found one thing in common to both lists:

Boxing.

HOW I DEVELOPED AND USED MY INTEREST _____

Boxing was a sport in which I had little or no interest before I met my husband.

As a medical student, he naturally spent most of his time in studies. This left little time for us when it came to mutual interests.

I was an enthusiastic golfer. My husband was an enthusiastic boxing fan. We had decided to share our interests as much as possible so that we could enjoy our time together to the fullest.

He, therefore, took up golf to please me.

I, in turn, started watching the fights—and going to them on occasion—to please him.

I found after a while, even though I had no great interest in boxing to begin with, that I was becoming more interested and beginning to enjoy and know a great deal about the sport.

Well, boxing was on my list of interests and it was on the list of topics which The $64,000 Question used for its contestants.

I plunged into a boxing encyclopedia. I spent five intensive weeks learning every nook and cranny of that huge book.

THE WEEKS OF STUDY BEGIN TO PAY OFF _____

I learned of boxers I had never dreamed existed. I learned of fights I had no idea had taken place. I accumulated facts about the history of the fight game that made me more and more fascinated as I went along.

These were, of course, facts that are ordinarily not important to the average boxing fan. But, I realized, if I wanted to go on the program and win the $64,000 prize, I had to have knowledge that was going to be greater than that of an average boxing fan.

Not only did I study the encyclopedia of boxing; I also read every other book and magazine article about the subject on which I could lay my hands.

I sought in my circle of friends and acquaintances persons who were interested in boxing. I realized that from each one I could gather facts and stories that would speed me on my way to a more-than-working knowledge of the history of boxing.

Whenever we were together, I veered the conversation to the sport and its history. Having friends interested in the subject forced me to keep up with them.

MAKING THE EGO PLAY ITS PART _____

At the beginning there was the competitive element brought into play in these conversations. I tried hard to acquire knowledge and display it.

Then there was the element of my own ego. As I became more sure of the detailed facts of the sport, I became proud of my ability to parade these data correctly at propitious moments.

As my enthusiasm increased, so did that of my circle of friends. They dug around for obscure facts in an effort to stump me. They brought around new people with similar interests.

In every way I was set to gain from this procedure—not only financially (as this had been my motivating plan) but in friendships. Our circle of friends increased and our life, that of my husband and myself, became fuller as a consequence.

When I felt that I had accumulated enough detailed knowledge on boxing so that I felt confident I could apply to the producers of the program, I applied. They were interested—and I was on my way.

HURDLING THE MAJOR BARRIER

In a preliminary interview I convinced them that I was able to get around in the subject of boxing. This seemed to please them greatly. They thought it was amusing that a lecturer in psychology—and a woman at that—was interested in boxing.

They found out to their satisfaction that my interest went far enough for me to make a competent contestant.

I went on the program, passed the first week's hurdle, and the game was under way.

The weeks went on; I answered question after question and reached plateau after plateau. Each week, spurred on by the amount of money I had already won, I decided to continue on to seek the big prize rather than go away with a lesser prize.

I felt that with the previous interest my husband had encouraged, the period of intensive study, and the continuing work I was doing as the program proceeded, I could gamble on losing all my winnings.

My confidence continued to build. So did my bankroll.

AN EVENING TO REMEMBER

Then came the climaxing night. I shall always remember getting into the isolation booth, waiting for the big question. I shall always remember the relief at finding that I knew the answer and hearing the words that told me my answer was correct.

I had won the big prize.

Since that night I have often been asked a question that is very indicative of how people think the memory reacts:

"Even though you know your subject, doesn't your mind go blank in a tense situation like that?"

My answer is simply:

"No. Not if you *know* your subject."

But I was convinced that if I could master the entire knowledge of one topic—enough to be able to compete in a contest as rigorous as The $64,000 Question program—anyone could master whatever knowledge he desired.

Remembering—that is, memory—had become too much of a joke with too many people.

MEMORY FAILURE IS NOT FUNNY

I recall one friend of mine who went to lectures given by a so-called memory expert. She attended the classes for months. I don't quite know what she learned, but I do remember her sister asking her one day:

"Has your memory really improved under the treatment you have been getting at these lectures? Do you remember things now?"

The answer was delightful, but it showed just what the student of memory had suffered and for how little. She said:

"Well, not exactly, but I have progressed so far that I can frequently remember that I have forgotten something—if I could only remember what it is."

Forgetfulness seems to strike everyone at some time or other. Yet there is no reason for it.

CARELESSNESS CAN BE COSTLY

A professor of mine once told a story on himself that showed how by sheer carelessness memory can slip away from us—if we allow it to.

This history expert was asked by the editors of a major encyclopedia to check a certain article that had been an important part of their books for many years.

The editors suggested to the professor that perhaps the article required some revision.

"Revision?" wrote back the professor indignantly, "why, this article is one of the most badly disorganized works I have ever seen. It is full of errors. It requires more than revision, it needs complete redoing."

Curious to see who had written such an "inaccurate" article for them originally, the editors checked through their files. They were flabbergasted to discover that the article had been written many years before by the professor in question.

He had forgotten that he had been the author.

INATTENTION IS MEMORY'S BUGABOO

Inattention is not an affliction found in professors alone. Memory failure, due purely to inattention, is a common ailment.

The late Dwight Morrow—lawyer, banker, ambassador, and senator—was the butt of many stories about his memory.

They tell of the time that he was sitting on a train, reading his newspaper earnestly, when the conductor asked for his ticket.

Frantically Mr. Morrow searched for it but he could not find it.

"Never mind, Mr. Morrow," said the conductor, who knew him well. "When you find it, mail it to the company. I'm certain you have it."

"Oh, I know I have it," exploded Mr. Morrow. "But what I want to know is, where in the world am I going?"

Another of the famous stories about Dwight Morrow involves a trip he was on and a wire he sent to his secretary.

It seems that when he got off the train at Grand Central Terminal in New York he had no idea why he was there. So he wired to his secretary:

"Why am I in New York? What am I supposed to do?"

His secretary replied that he was on his way to Princeton to deliver an address. And so he proceeded on his way.

YOU, TOO, CAN HAVE A SUCCESSFUL MEMORY _____

These stories may bring laughs—but actually forgetfulness is not funny.

There is no need for anyone to be forgetful.

There is no need for anyone to be unable to remember.

There is no need, once you have read the chapters that follow, for you not to make successful use of your memory powers—immediately.

My own story is only one of thousands that have happened every day.

It can be *you*—if you want it to.

PART ONE

HOW YOU CAN DO IT!

You must learn me how to remember!
Shakespeare: As You Like It.

1

THE MAGIC OF YOUR MEMORY

Memory is the treasury and guardian of all things.
Cicero: *De Oratore,* Book I.

It's right on the tip of my tongue!"

How many times have you been forced to say that—and then admit: "But I can't remember it!"

How many times have you searched and sought and probed into the far corners of your brain and not been able to remember something you needed at the exact moment when you needed it?

Your problem is, of course, not unique. Almost everyone suffers from memory trouble. It is probably mankind's most common failing.

But it can be cured!

You have within you, right now, the power to overcome your memory troubles.

You have the ability—*if you want to use it*—of developing your memory ten-fold *within ten days.*

You have been born with a great gift. This gift is memory. And you have only to *desire* to use it in order to bring into full play the remarkable faculties of your memory. It rests with you—and you alone—to be able to accomplish ends that you never before believed possible.

All with your memory!

What can a better memory mean to you?

1. *It can spell the difference between failure and success!*

2. It can open the door from the dark room of unhappiness into the bright palace of happiness.
3. It can carry you across the threshold of fear into the world of self-confidence.
4. It can banish the bugbear of indecision, the bugaboo of doubt, and the spectre of inferiority.

"All this, if I can improve my memory?"

I can just hear you skeptically ask that question. And while you may have reason to wonder at the power your memory can bring to you, you will soon be startled when you begin to use the great natural abilities that are already within you—abilities that await only awakening.

FROM TEN PERCENT TO ONE HUNDRED PERCENT _____

"Do you mean to say that even though I had a hard time remembering poetry at school, and I could never memorize a multiplication table, that I now can make something of my memory?"

That, in just those words, was the question put to me by a young friend of mine.

And it was that question that set me to realizing that she—and quite possibly you—may have overlooked the greatest power of the brain . . . the memory.

My answer is a bold **YES**. Yes, you can make something of your memory.

Yes, you can develop that wonderful power so that it will help you do wonderful things.

In the following pages I will show you how you can improve your memory powers ten-fold. This is not hocus-pocus. This is not trickery. This is simple fact, borne out by the long research and patient work of psychologists, medical men, and other men of science.

It was William James, one of the founders of psychology, who computed that, under normal circumstances, only about ten per cent of the potential mental capacity is developed in an individual.

"Only ten per cent?" I was once asked by a student with a quizzical frown of shock.

Only ten per cent!

And yet all the potential is there. You have the power within you to use the full hundred per cent of your brain capacity. You can make your memory work for you effectively—and, best of all, profitably.

MEMORY-EFFICIENCY: THE POWER TO REMEMBER _____

What most people fail to realize is that memory is a power that is perpetually in action. Without memory all experience would be useless: we could not reason, we could not judge, we could not conjecture, we could not even imagine.

Memory, then, is indispensable to us. And memory-efficiency is vital.

1. Without memory-efficiency many necessary things are left undone.
2. Without memory-efficiency many important things are never gained.
3. Without memory-efficiency much of life passes by and we never recognize it nor appreciate it.

Memory-efficiency is what this book will give you. It is the power to remember. As you read each chapter and learn how to improve your memory, how to make your memory *work for you* and how to enhance your life through your memory, you will day by day improve the powers of your memory-efficiency. Within ten days you will have discovered the power to remember successfully.

The great Dr. Samuel Johnson once wrote that "we owe to memory not only the increase of our knowledge, and our progress in rational inquiries, but many other intellectual pleasures. Indeed, almost all that we can be said to enjoy is past or future; the present is in perpetual motion, leaves us as soon as it arrives, ceases to be present before its presence is well perceived, and is only known to have existed by the effects which it leaves behind. The greatest part of our ideas arises, therefore, from the view before or behind us, and we are happy or miserable, according as we are affected by the survey of our life, or our prospect of future existence."

So it is that everything you do depends in some way on your memory. It is logical, therefore, to reason that everything you do can be accomplished with greater ease and greater efficiency. Everything hinges on your power to remember, successfully.

MEMORY'S ROLE IN LIFE _____

"Of course," you may say, "a good memory is important for an actor or a concert artist, but what is it going to do for me?"

Memory plays an extremely important role in the life of every businessperson and professional. It is also of everyday importance in the home. There is no one who cannot benefit by improving memory-efficiency.

Sometimes it is the smallest of things that bears remembering—and yet is forgotten.

They tell a story of the man who was hired to catalog every volume in the library of a large European city. He was a short man and he chose a rather thick volume to place on the chair he was going to use while he worked.

When he had completed his great work, it was discovered that his vast index had one glaring error. He had forgotten to include the single volume on which he had been sitting for thirty years!

Everything of importance to your work and your everyday living habits should be rememberable.

Look at what an increased memory can mean to a person in business. The merchant who can immediately bring to mind the names of wholesalers and customers, buying and selling prices for every item, pertinent data about employees, is far more efficient than the one who is uncertain.

A banker, for instance, who can recall even such a small detail as what a customer's signature looks like is an asset to the organization. The manager of my bank once told me of a bank clerk who was given a check by a customer's wife. He knew her, but the signature on the check seemed wrong.

After telling the manager of his suspicions, he calmly asked her if she would go in to see the manager. After a short chat, the manager touched on the subject of the check.

"Oh, the check is all right," the woman said. "There is more than enough money in the account."

"But the signature," prompted the manager.

"That's the way Harold always signs his name, isn't it?" asked the woman.

"Possibly," agreed the manager, "but is this your husband's writing?"

"Well, not exactly," she admitted, "but it's as close as I could come to it."

A humorous story; but it could have been a tragic one. The employer or employee with the *power to remember successfully* is a priceless asset to a business.

THE BUSINESS OF MEMORY

People who are uncertain about details are bound to make mistakes simply because they cannot remember figures or other data accurately. They waste their own time and that of the other members of their firm. On top of that they waste the time of the people they deal with.

Instead of having every detail at their fingertips, they have to prod their brains unnecessarily and hunt for information.

I know a key employee of a large corporation who has often marvelled at the memory-efficiency of other people. "Oh, if only I could snap out facts and figures at a sales conference, instead of having to call my secretary to get them for me and holding up the meeting," he once said to me.

There are many reasons why this executive failed in the task he wanted to perform. Yet he can now do as he once wished.

By developing his memory-efficiency and successfully using his power to remember in the way outlined in the chapters that follow, he now amazes the other executives at sales meetings by having every vital piece of data at tongue's end.

How can an improved memory affect, let us say, a salesperson? Well, let us imagine a salesperson with a good memory and one with an average memory. The salesperson whose memory-efficiency is at its highest, uses powers of remembering successfully. That person knows the name of the buyer when they meet, recalls details about the buyer's family, personal hobbies, likes and dislikes. As a result, they are able to talk about these personal and intimate things.

What will this accomplish? It breaks down the first difficult minutes of conversation. It enables the salesperson to establish what psychologists call "rapport" with the buyer. That is to say, they establish a personal contact. That, as any salesperson will tell you, is the most important tool in successfully conducting a business involving sales.

MAKING MEMORY WORK FOR YOU _____

So, immediately, the salesperson with the memory-efficiency finds that the power to remember successfully is working. In addition that salesperson has a second advantage over the one with the average memory. That salesperson is ready to give offhand all the information about the product that the buyer will require and may ask for. This can be done without hesitation, without delay, without hemming and hawing. Such an approach makes the salesperson sound confident and shows the buyer that the salesperson is impressed with the importance of the product.

The third advantage in having the power to remember successfully is that once the salesperson has prepared a sales argument properly, it can be kept in mind at all times—something that a competitor with average memory cannot do.

How does memory-efficiency help professional people—the doctor, the lawyer?

Well, let us take your own individual relationship with your doctor. How much more confidence have you in a physician who, when you meet on the street unexpectedly, can call you by name, ask about your last illness or ailment, and inquire in the same fashion about every member of your family?

Of course, your respect for this person is bound to be high. You know this doctor has a keener interest in you than the physician who forgets about you the minute you leave the office and have paid the bill.

ADVANTAGES OF PAST EXPERIENCE _____

Look at the advantage surgeons with successful memory-efficiency have. Surgeons often have to work quickly with little time to prepare. They must remember the exact history of the case at hand and of similar cases if they are to apply the correct treatment.

If they have encountered similar cases in their own practices, then their difficulties are lessened, for memory more easily retains things that we have perceived with our own eyes or that are connected with our own selves. But to remember only their own cases is not enough for surgeons. They have to remember similar cases described in medical literature.

Of course, doctors' memories may sometimes lead them astray. Doctors tell the story of a surgeon being awakened in the middle of the night by a man claiming his wife had just had an appendicitis attack.

"But," the surgeon said sleepily over the phone, "that's impossible. I took your wife's appendix out five years ago. Nobody ever has a second appendix."

"Certainly," the man replied, "but a man can have a second wife. I remarried after my wife died three years ago!"

Can a better memory help a lawyer?

If you have had the good fortune never to be involved in a lawsuit, you must at least have known someone who was, or you may have read in the newspapers of trials where the memory of counsel has proved to be invaluable.

In the first place, like the doctor, the lawyer has to remember similar cases. Legal precedents, as they are called, play a very important part in the deciding of a case, for what a judge has said in the past often determines what another judge will say in the future.

MEMORY-EFFICIENCY IN THE LAW COURT

But lawyers must have all these precedents at their fingertips. They can't suddenly send some member of their staff off to the library to get volumes of past decisions and to search for the one they think fits the case. They must be able to rattle off the precedents at the drop of an objection. A lawyer's power to remember successfully has to be developed to the highest pitch.

I remember once reading how one lawyer's memory-efficiency served his client well. After one witness in the case recited her story, all looked black for this lawyer's client. The jury, and even the judge, scowled at the defendant in the case.

But the lawyer, sensing something false in the witness' story, quietly approached the witness stand and in a gentle way asked the witness to repeat the story. This she did and again the client shrank in his seat under the glares of the jury. The lawyer made the witness tell the story a third time and then as she finished, asked:

"Didn't you forget one word?"

The witness paused for a moment and then admitted to having forgotten one word.

"Well," said the lawyer with a slow smile, "tell the story *again* and this time put the word in."

It was obvious to the jury now, as the story was told for the fourth time, that it was a story learned by heart. And it was thus that a lawyer with a highly developed memory-efficiency managed to save his client from an unwarranted and serious punishment.

The lawyer's keen memory made him realize that the story had been repeated by rote.

MEMORY-EFFICIENCY IN EVERYDAY LIFE

But memory-efficiency is equally important in your everyday personal life.

How many times have you had something "right on the tip of your tongue"? Isn't it embarrassing to introduce friends and find that you can't remember their names? Or have you, perhaps, had the even more embarrassing experience of an acquaintance of mine who could not remember the names of both persons he was introducing—and he had known both quite well for a period of many years!

How many times have you had a series of errands to do and returned home only to find that you had forgotten the most important of them—or perhaps more than one? The irritation, or the continuing aggravation, of such duplication of effort accused by failure of your memory-efficiency is probably familiar to you.

A poor memory is more than just an irritation or an annoyance. It can be a serious handicap. But it is one that can be overcome by a serious approach to the problem and by intelligent effort to increase the power of your remembering.

You have probably often talked about your memory, but have never done anything about improving it. Now is your chance. Now you hold within your hands the key to improving your memory-efficiency and improving it to the utmost limits of its capacity.

THE REASON TO REMEMBER

In the chapters that follow, you will learn how to determine your reason for learning. Science has demonstrated over and over that the greater the motive there is for learning, the greater is the power to learn.

You will learn how to determine your motivation and how to

channel it. In this way you will not lose any of your power of remembering by having it tapped off through lack of organization.

You will learn to overcome your moods so that you will not become a slave to them. Application to a task need not follow a mood—you can work despite your mood or outside distractions.

You will learn how your brain works during periods of "rest." This enables you to break up your concerted effort and to gain by these "breaks."

You will learn how your brain functions and how it retains its powers. You will discover that the brain does not fatigue and that there is a way to uncover its maximum efficiency.

You will learn to make your approach to memory meaningful. It is easier to learn something that has meaning to you, and it is easier to retain it. This is one of the important tricks to improving your memory.

You will learn how to set goals for yourself and how to reach them. You will be shown how you improve your memory-efficiency faster the closer you get to your goal.

You will learn how to reward yourself for having reached pre-set levels along the road to success. You will discover how to set levels for yourself.

You will learn the tricks of timing in improving your memory capacity. In this way you will be able to take advantage of precious minutes in every day.

You will learn the "Bird's-Eye View" method which will enable you to commit vast quantities of knowledge to memory. This makes it simple to do a great deal of work in the easiest and most efficient manner.

You will learn the key to a permanent memory.

You will learn the importance of forgetting.

This sounds like an arduous program. It is not! The beauty of improving your power to remember successfully is that it is easily done. It requires only the use of the right technique.

The right technique is what you are going to be given in the following pages.

You will have to co-operate with me. Just reading this book is not going to increase your power to remember from ten per cent to one hundred per cent. It requires more than mere reading. It requires you to use the techniques of memory-efficiency.

But you are not going to have to wait until you reach the end of the book to achieve results.

EACH CHAPTER BRINGS YOU CLOSER _____

Every chapter of this book has been designed to bring you one step closer to achieving your aim of having a successful memory. Every chapter will increase your power to remember by another ten-percent step along the *Memory Meter.* Your goal is memory-efficiency in ten days.

All through the chapters that follow, you will find experiments and examples in which you are to participate. If you want to help yourself to a successful memory, participate! They are designed with a purpose. They help you make it easy for yourself to practice the lessons you are learning in the steps up the ladder to a peak of memory-efficiency.

Facing you are all the joys and benefits of the power to remember successfully.

> *Your stumbling blocks will be overcome . . .*
>
> *Your lack of confidence will be mastered . . .*
>
> *Your ability to influence people will be increased . . .*
>
> *Your future happiness will be enhanced . . .*
>
> *. . . all because of your power to remember successfully.*

PART TWO

THE
TEN DAYS

Memory: the library of the mind.
Francis Fauvel-Gourand: *Mnemo-technic Dictionary.*

YOUR MEMORY— WHAT IS IT?

Memory, the warder of the brain.
Shakespeare: *Macbeth.*

What is this thing we call the memory?

It is, without a single doubt, one of the most wonderful things possessed by the human. Without memory we would be unable to do most of the everyday things we now look upon as routine and of almost no importance.

And yet—wonderful though we realize it is—we use it all the time without ever stopping to consider just *what* it is.

We go to far greater pains to understand our automobiles, our television sets, even our washing machines, refrigerators, and electric broilers. We learn what makes these inventions work so that we can make better and more efficient use of them.

But we are inclined to take far too casually nature's most intricate invention. Our memory is the prime function of a highly complicated machine that man has never been able to duplicate completely—the brain.

Your brain is a delicate and fragile thing; to protect it, nature set the brain inside a hard bone casing. Yet this little bundle of tissue is responsible for every action you make, every word you say, every thought you think.

TWO KINDS OF MEMORY _____

Your memory plays a part in two ways.

> *1. You repeat something you have done before (the automatic function of directly using something you have learned).*
>
> *2. You reason out an action based on past experience (the nonautomatic function of indirectly using things you have learned).*

So you see how important your memory is. Without it you would be able to accomplish little. Your every action would be of the trial-and-error type—without your being able to anticipate the results by "remembering" the results of previous trials. The outcome of your every action would depend solely on chance.

"Oh, sure, I have a memory," a young schoolteacher once complained to me, "but it is a bad memory!"

That is too common a complaint and yet it is one that has absolutely no foundation in fact. *There is no such thing as a "bad memory."*

The only thing wrong with the teacher's memory was the technique she employed in using it. That is the greatest fault most people have who insist that their memories are "bad."

By the same token there is no such thing as a "good memory." I have often heard people exclaim over the "remarkable feats" of some person or other who displays powers of memory with trick or showy facility.

It is not "good memory"—it is only good technique of memory.

THE TECHNIQUE OF MEMORY _____

The difference between the person who employs memory efficiently and the one who doesn't is technique.

There is nothing startling about the idea of technique. It is technique that is required to make any person "good" at anything.

> *1. You cannot become a good boxer without acquiring and working at the techniques of boxing.*

2. You cannot become a good dancer without studying and applying the techniques of dancing.
3. You cannot become a good musician without learning the techniques of playing the instrument you have chosen.
4. You cannot become a good typist without practicing the techniques of using a typewriter.

Whether it's tennis, or golf, or swimming, or skiing, or painting, or sculpting, or writing, or singing, or acting . . . *technique is vital.*

Technique is acquired; it can be learned, developed, and applied.

And so it is with memory. There is a technique to employing your memory. Having learned it, you will have learned to put your memory to greater and better use.

The proof of this contention is simple.

EMPLOYING THE TECHNIQUE _____

Take, for example, actors. You have no doubt heard of some actors being called "quick studies." That means that they can learn a role for a new play very rapidly. That is an advantage since it means that producers and directors can expect no difficulty from them when they hire them for productions. It means that they can spend more time developing the characterization of the part, rather than wasting excessive time in learning the words they have to speak.

Or take the case of politicians. Those in political life who create the best impression on their constituents are the ones who, along with showing good sense in the activities to which they have been elected, can remember the names of most of their constituents. In addition, they remember facts about their families, their businesses, convincing each voter that the person they have voted for has a personal interest in them.

Is it coincidence, then, that has given these actors and politicians "good memories"? No, it is not a matter of "good memory" or of "bad memory"—it is purely a matter of technique.

The secrets of technique and the keys to using this technique are what the following chapters of this book are going to unfold to you.

By improving your technique of remembering, you will increase what I call your memory-efficiency. It will be increased tenfold. Using your power to remember successfully will bring you a gain from ten per cent to one hundred per cent in the use of your memory-efficiency.

You now have learned an essential fact about the development of memory.

It is based on good technique.

WHAT IS MEMORY?

Now, to get back to our initial question: what is memory?

The scientific theories of memory are in a sense complicated. For one thing, scientists do not quite agree on just how memory works. One group—including physicians, psychologists and biologists—thinks that memory works in one fashion. Another group—including members of the same three professions—thinks the memory works in another fashion.

But then the question is probably too broad and too general for any one simple answer. After all, the physicist does not pretend to know what electrical charges are. Nor does the botanist claim to know what the growth of plants is.

Rather than go into the many complicated theories about what the memory is, it might be more clear to compare the memory to a giant filing system.

Your brain can be likened to a large series of filing cabinets into which every single thing that you see, hear, and read is immediately categorized and filed. Whether or not it is filed in a manner that makes it readily available to you again *when you want it* depends entirely on you.

You have the power to select those things that you want to have "filed" for future use—whether in the immediate future or distant future. You also determine which of the things you perceive about you are to be "filed" in what you might call the discard file.

The things you want to remember, those things your technique will help you to file. In that way they will be readily accessible. That is your power to remember successfully. That is the power that the techniques you learn in reading this book will give to you—in simple, everyday language.

The things that belong in the "file and forget" category, those will be taken care of by your brain, too. You will learn to utilize the technique of placing such matter where it will not clutter up the active section of your vast filing system.

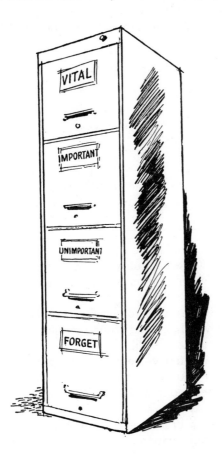

Without conscious effort on your part your brain files away the facts that interest you—or that you want to remember—in readily accessible compartments. Those things that hold little or no interest for you—or that you don't want to remember—are tucked far away in the recesses of the "back room."

Let us take a simple, everyday example of how your brain performs this function for you.

WHAT THINGS DID YOU REMEMBER TODAY? _____

Sometime today or yesterday you probably did some walking. It may have been a long walk, or perhaps you just went to the corner to pick up a newspaper or a loaf of bread. No matter, long or short walk, think back to it for a moment. Now take a pencil and answer the following questions:

Did you meet anyone that you knew? _____

What was that person or persons wearing? _____

_____

Did you talk to anyone while you were out? _____

What did you talk about? _____

_____

Did you pass by any stores on the way? _____

What was displayed in the windows of those shops? _____

_____

Think carefully before you write your answer for each of the questions. Try to remember every detail you can.

Now read the answers and let us evaluate a basic fact about your brain and your memory.

You will notice that you have remembered some things in some detail. Other things you have had some recollection of. Still others you have not remembered at all.

Can you explain why you have been able to remember some things and not others? Did you consciously try to remember the things that you did remember and try to forget those things that you cannot now recall?

The answer is no. Your brain was remembering—and disremembering—for you quite automatically.

WHY DID YOU REMEMBER THEM? _____

Those things that are of interest to you, those are the things you have remembered. Right?

Those things that have little or no interest for you, those are the things that you barely remembered or have completely forgotten. True?

It's a matter of things that interest you.

If you stopped to talk with anyone, you probably remembered the topic of conversation if it was one that interested you: perhaps your hobby, your children, politics.

If what you talked about generally bores you—the movie your acquaintance saw the night before, some gossip about someone you barely know—then the chances are you have not the slightest inkling what it was you spent five minutes standing on the street corner chatting about.

Again, it's a matter of things in which you are interested.

If you passed any stores, you peeked into the shop windows—if only fleetingly—and saw things that interested you. Perhaps it was a hat shop and the latest creation caught your eye—even though you've stopped to look at it before. Or it was a sporting goods store and that fishing pole was still in the window.

You've recalled those things—because they hold some interest for you.

Maybe the store you passed was the grocery down the street. Did you notice whether the window was filled with oranges or apples? Was there a special on canned green peas this week?

If you were hungry, the chances are that this window display caught your attention.

If you weren't hungry, you most likely were not interested in what was being advertised in a grocery window and therefore have perhaps only a vague—if any—idea of what you saw.

SPECIAL INTERESTS STIMULATE MEMORY _____

Your own special interests will determine what you are going to remember—unconsciously—without any effort on your part.

A story of an Army man returning from long duty overseas points up clearly how a "special" interest will unconsciously stimulate the memory.

This soldier flew back from duty and was met at the airport by his fiancée. While they were awaiting his luggage, he pointed out the good-looking stewardess who had been on the plane.

"That's Miss Tracy," the young soldier said to his fiancee.

"How do you happen to know her name?" the soldier's girl asked.

The Army man explained that it was listed, along with the

names of the pilot and co-pilot, on the door of the plane's cockpit.

The fiancée's next question floored the soldier.

"Dear," she asked, "what was the pilot's name?"

So you see that your memory automatically functions in a way that helps you remember in spite of yourself. You remember the things you want to remember. You forget the things that interest you least.

With this basic fact in mind you are able now to refute for yourself the theory of "good memory" and "bad memory."

That is how the technique of memory-efficiency works. If you want to remember, you are going to have to improve your memory technique and make it good. You are going to have to replace the ineffectual technique you now have and use.

Memory, then, is much like a giant filing system run efficiently by your brain.

It works not at all unlike those electronic brains that catalog information and keep handiest those things that are most frequently required.

If you want to remember something, you must learn to "file" it in a handy place.

If you don't want to remember it, you must learn to use the file-and-forget faculty of the brain so that it is "filed" far back in the seldom-used corners.

YOUR MEMORY METER

It is all a matter of technique—technique that you will be shown and will learn to use effectively in the chapters that follow.

The techniques of memory, of the power to remember successfully, will be charted for you as you go along.

At the end of every chapter in this section you will find a MEMORY METER. This is a chart of your progress toward learning how to remember successfully—a chart of your progress toward increasing your memory-efficiency ten-fold.

As you read each chapter you will increase your memory-efficiency another ten per cent. This gain will be recorded on your MEMORY METER. Within ten days you will have mastered the power of remembering successfully.

Now you have learned that, according to James, you have a normal usage of ten per cent of your brain when it comes to memory. This is the foundation upon which you are going to build your memory-efficiency.

MEMORY METER

100%
90%
80%
70%
60%
50%
40%
30%
20%
10% Normal Usage

3

The Second Day

YOUR MEMORY MOTIVE

The memory strengthens as you lay burdens upon it.
Thomas De Quincey: *Confessions of an English Opium-Eater.*

One important factor will lead you onto the road of memory betterment.

That single element is the key to your entire program of increasing your memory-efficiency ten-fold.

I call it your Memory Motive.

Every single action you perform, every moment of every day, is motivated—something impels you to do it. There is a reason, a need, a desire; whatever it is, it can be defined as a motive.

So it must be with memory-efficiency. You must have a motive.

The dictionary defines a motive as "that which induces a person to act." As a cold, hard dictionary definition, it fills the bill. But to paint a clearer picture of what a motive is and how vital it is in your program of memory-efficiency, let me define it as akin to the fuel you use in your automobile.

Without fuel you lack the driving power. Without the driving power, you are without the necessary push to go anywhere. If you want to go in a particular direction, you must have the power. That power—that fuel—is motive.

Your first step, then, in setting out on the road to an improved memory is:

Establish your Memory Motive.

WHAT MOTIVES ARE THERE?

Motives are of two kinds—the unlearned and the learned.

The unlearned motives impel the automatic actions of your everyday life. You rarely think of them, or even realize that they exist. They just occur: the desire for sleep, the feeling of hunger and thirst, the sex drive.

These are the motives common to all life. They are inborn. They appear and we are impelled to satisfy them.

The learned, or acquired, motives take many forms. All your everyday interests motivate all your everyday activities. They are motives for social approval—common social motives: the desire to win in competition with others, the desire to gain praise, the desire to avoid censure from those we respect, the desire to gain self-respect, among many.

The incentives that can be counted on to call forth these motives vary from person to person and from situation to situation. Money, for example, is an incentive that has a widespread appeal. That is because money can satisfy many motives at once. The desire for security is an impelling motive common to many people. The longing for a sense of personal worth is more intensified today than ever before.

The desire for social approval will, perhaps, induce you to learn to play bridge—or the lastest card-game craze. Or it will get you to take dance lessons in the latest fad so that you can "run with the crowd."

The desire for a home and a family will motivate you to find a spouse. This might entail many changes in your everyday way of life. Yet you hardly hesitate to make changes, if they will help you satisfy the motive.

Your interests will lead you to take a greater part in the activities you enjoy. You may be a baseball fan and will, therefore, acquire a bookful of knowledge about the great American sport. You might be a jazz lover and seriously study music to understand the roots of modern rhythms and melodies.

Whatever it is you are interested in or want, a motive is the push to help you acquire—be it knowledge, wealth, health, happiness.

DESIRE HELPS YOU ACQUIRE _____

You have only to *desire.*

Having stepped on this "starter," you have set the engine of your brain in motion. It will not cease until it works out how to *acquire* that which you desire.

The mere fact that you are reading this book at this moment indicates that you have the one basic requirement for accomplishing the betterment of your memory-efficiency.

Your need to improve your memory was the motive that led you to read this book.

Why have you a need to improve your memory? What is the basic incentive that has stimulated this motive? Think about this. Now write it down in this space:

Here, then, is the *reason* you are reading this book.

This reason is the very thing that you must utilize to help you improve your memory-efficiency and thus lead yourself to the power to remember successfully.

This reason is your Memory Motive.

The greater this reason is, the greater is the motive. Thereby you have formulated the first rule of memory:

Memory increases in proportion to motive.

Read that sentence again! Read it aloud! Repeat it now, without looking at the book.

Now get a pencil. Write that sentence down on the following line:

_____

That is a rule that has been demonstrated over and over again.

PROOF OF THE PUDDING _____

One of the most interesting—and entertaining—experiments that psychologists have employed to show how this rule works involves a chimpanzee and a vending machine.

The chimpanzee is not fed for some time. When natural hunger pangs become apparent, it is placed in a room with a slot machine filled with grapes. The chimpanzee is also left some poker chips that operate the machine and "pay off" in grapes.

The animal's hunger will lead it to experiment until it discovers that by placing a chip in the slot of the machine it can get food.

Its basic hunger motive helps its memory to acquire a new skill—one that without motive it would never have learned.

The same chimpanzee can again be put through the experiment. This time, however, the poker chips are various colors. The white chip will cause the slot machine to give up one grape; the blue chip will give the animal two grapes.

In a short time, the chimpanzee learns to distinguish between the colors in terms of the amount of food each produces for it. It soon will always choose the blue chip.

The basic desire for food, here, is the reason for remembering. The chimpanzee learns through trial and error, but once it has figured out the solution to the machinery, it is set.

REPETITION ALONE IS NOT THE ANSWER

Some critics have said that it is only repetition that causes the chimpanzee to remember what to do to get food.

That, unfortunately, is not so. Were it as simple as that, your memory problems would be solved in one fell swoop.

Repetition alone is not the answer!

Certainly, when you learned poetry in your school days you managed to remember the lines by repeating them over and over. But honestly, how much of that poetry do you remember today?

You may say that you learned the poetry many years ago and you have not had the opportunity, or the need, to use it since.

All right. What about things you do every day of your life? How well does the repetition of these actions help you to remember?

For example: How many times a day do you use the telephone? How often in every week do you dial numbers?

The chances are that your answer ranges into the hundreds.

Now, without looking at your telephone dial, answer this question:

What letter or letters of the alphabet are missing on the

dial? You have, by your own admission, claimed that you use the phone countless times in a year and untold times over the span of your life. Here is repetition of a kind rarely found in any other field of activity.

Yet, did you know that there are only twenty-four letters on most telephones? Did you know that the letter Q has always been left off and the letter Z does not appear on recent model phones either?

The value of repetition alone, then, is questionable.

MOTIVATION IS THE KEY

Its value comes when it is combined with motivation. When you have reason to remember, that power can be aided by repetition.

Therefore, you have the second rule of memory: *Motive plus repetition equals retention.*

Now that you have acquired the two principal rules of a better memory, you are ready to improve your memory-efficiency.

A few pages back you wrote down your motive for improving your memory-efficiency. This is going to be the key to helping you gain the power to remember successfully.

To channel your Memory Motive so that its powers are increased, you should have filled in the answer to that question. If you want to reach the object of your desires quickly, simply, and with the greatest possible success, you should have listed your motive.

Now you have to make a list of:

1. *The reasons you have for desiring this end-result.*
2. *The advantages you will gain by improving your memory in this fashion.*

You read my story in the introductory chapter at the beginning of this book. Do you remember how I had come to a major decision? Do you remember my Memory Motive?

We required money so that my husband could continue with his medical studies. I, then, made a list just as I have outlined above. Go back and reread that introductory chapter now.

MY MEMORY MOTIVE LIST _____

With the details fresh in your mind, here is what my list looked like.

MEMORY MOTIVE: Money

REASONS: Having taken a leave of absence from teaching to have a child, our family income is cut. To help my husband continue with his medical studies and still play my proper role as a mother, I have to find a way to earn money from a source other than teaching and in a manner that will give me a considerable sum quickly.

ADVANTAGES: My duties as a mother will not be interrupted. My husband will be able to continue his studies and be graduated on schedule. My home life, then, will not suffer, and our future will be made secure.

Now, in the space provided, do the same thing. Prepare for yourself a list of reasons and advantages tying in your Memory Motive with the result desired.

YOUR MEMORY MOTIVE LIST _____

Memory Motive:

Reasons:

Advantages:

EVERYBODY HAS MEMORY MOTIVES _____

The Memory Motive is an everyday occurrence in the lives of countless people around you. My own case was not unusual. But it pointed up to me how many other people in my circle of friends and acquaintances were motivated in the same way.

A young man I know learned to speak Swedish—and it is far from an easy language to speak—in record time. Why? Simply because he had met a woman during a business trip to Sweden, with whom he fell in love. He decided that he wanted to marry her.

His quick acquisition and his eventual mastery of the language led him along the path of happiness that he sought.

A woman I went to college with wanted to be a newspaper reporter. She hoped to get a job in the city where her family lived—despite the fact that it was a metropolis, and there was little chance for a person with no experience to start on one of its papers.

She took her courage in hand, however, and went to see the managing editor of one of the city's newspapers. After questioning her about her background and experience, he suddenly said:

"Well, we've been wanting to have a woman working in the sports department. Go out to the stadium tomorrow afternoon and cover the football game. If you do a good job, you're hired."

My friend had attended a few college football games during her four years at the university, but her knowledge of the game was practically nil. She cheered when the home team seemed to be gaining ground, and cheered louder when they scored. But she had very little knowledge as to what was happening on the field.

There was only one thing to do. She wanted the job—not particularly in the sports department, but she knew that once she was hired by the paper she could try to get transferred later to the department of her choosing. She went to the library and took out every book there was on football.

She read and studied until she knew all the fine fine points of the game, all the terminology, and most of the classical plays of the sport's history.

A STRONG MEMORY MOTIVE MAKES SUCCESS _____

Her Memory Motive was strong. She went to the stadium the next afternoon and turned in a brilliant job of covering the football game.

The job was hers and with it came her eventual opportunity to transfer to the job of her choosing. She now is labor expert on a large daily newspaper in an important mideastern manufacturing city.

Another young man I once met was working as an assistant librarian on the staff of a weekly magazine. He wanted to improve his position and so he studied the prospects of transferring to another department in the magazine.

His survey showed that he would fare best if he were employed on the editorial staff. Next, he wondered to which editorial department he should try to transfer. As everyone on the magazine's editorial staff was an expert, he reviewed his own interests.

Highest on his list was music. He loved classical music and listened to it constantly. But his knowledge of composers, their works, instrumentation and technique, was slim. So he set about studying all he could about music.

He acquired a new set of friends whose main interest was music. He listened to all they had to say, factually and critically. He asked questions and found that his friends were not annoyed but flattered. As he learned more about the subject, he tested his wings. He joined in their discussions. He discovered that the more he talked about what he knew in the field, the better he remembered all his knowledge.

Thus, he employed the third rule of memory—*memory retention increases in proportion to memory use.* This young man soon enabled himself to acquire the knowledge that eventually resulted in his being hired as the magazine's music critic. He holds that position today—and is highly respected in the field.

THE FIRST THREE RULES

You have now learned, therefore, the first three rules of memory:

> *1. Memory increases in proportion to the motive.*
> *2. Motive plus repetition equals retention.*
> *3. Memory retention increases in proportion to memory use.*

So you see how important the Memory Motive is—it is the key to the very first rule you have to learn.

You have to set a goal for yourself. The very *action* of setting a goal sets up the *reaction* of accomplishment. There is my personal case with The $64,000 Question; there is the case of the young man who wanted to marry the Swedish woman; there is the case of the woman who wanted to be a newspaper reporter; there is the case of the librarian who wanted to improve his position.

There are thousands of such cases—thousands of persons who have learned how the setting of a goal helps to accomplish that goal.

Your power to improve your memory-efficiency is generated in yourself by the very action of setting a goal.

Kurt Lewin, the well-known psychologist, showed by experiment what he called his "tension" theory; that is, a "tendency toward completion" that persists and determines the nature of a person's behavior until a certain activity is completed.

Lewin contended that once people start to do something, they are compelled to finish it. So it is that you may work at a jigsaw or crossword puzzle until it is completed. Or you will continue to eat until your plate is empty, regardless of whether you were hungry enough to eat all the food. Or children will beg to be allowed to complete a game, even though they are thoroughly exhausted.

Lewin's theory is that the beginning of a concentrated activity creates the "tension"; and this "tension" is not relieved until the activity has been terminated by the attainment of the goal.

WHEN MEMORY FUNCTIONS BEST

Working on the basis of Lewin's theory, studies were made among various groups of people that led to convincing proof that the memory functions best when on its way to the accomplishment of a goal.

The studies involved a series of tests comprising various tasks each of which would take some time. These tasks, for example, required modeling an animal in clay, filling a sheet of paper by drawing crosses over its entire surface, counting backwards from 55 to 17, solving matchstick puzzles, naming a dozen cities all beginning with a particular letter of the alphabet, stringing beads on a thread.

Each task required between three and five minutes to complete and few could be completed in less than two minutes. The persons tested were permitted to complete half of the tasks assigned. Each of the remaining tasks was interrupted mid-way by the sudden introduction of a new task. The tasks thus interrupted remained unfinished; the persons were not permitted to go back and resume them.

The order of the tasks, completed and uncompleted, was random so that the persons taking the test did not learn when to expect an interruption. Nor was the reason for any interruption ever told, so that none had any idea that interruption was the major condition of the experiment.

At the end of the program of tasks, the people were asked to recall what tasks they had been assigned to do in the test. They listed as many tasks as they could remember. The experimenter noted privately which of the listed tasks had been completed and which had not.

A GOAL IN SIGHT HELPS MEMORY

In every group tested, adult or child, the members managed to recall two uncompleted tasks for every one they remembered of those they had been given time to finish.

In addition, the persons all had a strong resistance to interruption and a decided tendency to resume an interrupted task after finishing the task that had intervened.

With a goal in sight—in this case completion of a task—the memory functions better than when there is no goal, or motive. This experiment is especially interesting in view of the fact that a longer time was spent on completed tasks than on uncompleted ones.

So you must channel your motives by setting a goal, and reinforce them by finding new friends who have similar interests and motives. While you are on the way to reaching that goal, your memory capacity will be increased ten per cent.

Your goal—your Memory Motive—is your first step in reaching perfect memory-efficiency.

Remember:

Memory increases in proportion to motive.

Motive plus repetition equals retention.

Memory retention increases in proportion to memory use.

MEMORY METER

100%
90%
80%
70%
60%
50%
40%
30%
20%   Memory Motive
10%   Normal Usage

4 *The Third Day*

MASTERING YOUR MOODS

Method is the mother of memory.
Thomas Fuller: *History of the Worthies of England.*

> *"Oh, I'm not in the mood to do anything now!"*
> *"I just don't feel like working today!"*
> *"I'd rather do something else at the moment!"*
> *"That can be done just as well later as now!"*

Do these excuses sound familiar to you? They *are* excuses—there are no two ways about it. They are the reasons you give to yourself when you have allowed yourself to become what I call a *Mood Slave.*

Being a Mood Slave is no different than being a procrastinator. "Putting off," no matter what the reason, is poor policy. Today is the best time to do anything. Now is the right time to start—and continue—your work in bettering your power to remember successfully.

Not being "in the mood" to do things you have to do is no more a legitimate excuse for delaying until tomorrow than is the now-familiar slogan on the wall of a Washington legislator's office:

> *"I'll do it tomorrow—I've made enough mistakes today."*

The publisher of one of this country's best fiction writers tells a story about this author that shows how delay is costly. The author is quoted as saying about his technique:

"First, I clean my typewriter," he said. "Then I go through my shelves and return all borrowed books. Then I play with my children. Then, if it's warm, I go for a swim. Then I find some friends to have a drink with. By then, it's time to clean the typewriter again."

SCIENCE SHOWS MOODS
AND ABILITY UNCONNECTED

Scientists, in many experiments, have definitely shown that there is no connection whatsoever between your "mood" and your "ability" to do good work.

In fact, probably much to your own surprise, you may find that you can accomplish more on the days you consider yourself "not in the mood" than you can on the days when you awaken "rarin' to go."

There is no need to allow yourself to become a slave to your moods—you must master them.

"But how?" was the simple question put to me by a student one day.

A very simple question, yes—but a vital one in taking your next step to accomplishing a successful memory.

THE FIRST STEP

Since you know that you can accomplish as much, and perhaps more, when you apply yourself independently of your feelings, the first step to mastering your moods is:

Recognize that you are being side-tracked by nothing more than a whim.

Catering to a mood is exactly that: giving in to a whim. It may be a desire to start reading that novel you have had lying around for days. It may be a suspicion there is something you might want to see on television. It may be a yearning to gossip over the telephone with your best friend. It may be anything else that will delay you.

No matter in what form it manifests itself, it is only a mood-enslaving monster keeping you from your set task.

Master the monster, master the mood. Admit to yourself you are only delaying the undertaking of a task you are afraid may be tedious, boring, or difficult.

If you are going to increase your power to remember successfully, you must do it now—without delay.

You have taken the first step:

Recognize that you are being side-tracked by nothing more than a whim.

THE SECOND STEP

Now comes the second step:

Immediately set about doing what you have set for yourself.

There can be no delays now! You have admitted the existence of a snare that seeks to keep you from your work. So don't fall into that snare even for a moment.

If you as much as stall for a second, you have set foot into the trap that the mood-enslaving monster has baited for you. If you don't get down to the task right away, you have given in—even if it is for a minute or two. Today's minute is bound to grow into tomorrow's hour. Tomorrow's hour will quickly grow into next week's day.

Before you realize what has happened, you will have become a slave to your moods, instead of their master.

Remember:

Immediately set about doing what you have set for yourself.

THE THIRD STEP

Third—and this step is equally as important as the others:

Continue at your task until it is completed.

Don't feel that just because you have taken the first two steps of becoming a Mood Master that you can let down. Letting down is not the right reward. You deserve a reward—but we will discuss this later—and the reward must not be a relaxation from the task.

People who take the first two steps but not the last are much like alcoholics who decide one day to go straight home from work without stopping for a drink. With steadfast determination they pass every bar and tavern along the route. They do not pause for a moment, not even to remember that every day in the past they have stopped for a drink in at least one place. Finally, safely past the last bar before reaching home, they stop. Then they smile in satisfaction and turn back to reward themself with "just one little drink" for having "accomplished" this task.

Remember:

Continue at your task until it is completed.

With these three rules for overcoming mood, you have no excuse to remain a Mood Slave. The tomorrow to which we put things off is always more than twenty-four hours away. This is its horrible trouble.

MOOD AND CREATIVENESS _____

"Does a person really work better despite the feelings of the moment?"

I know that question is bothering you, because I have had it asked me in many ways, and many times.

But, think for a moment and consider what would happen if all the creative people in this world were to wait for the spirit to move them. The sum total of our advancement would be far less than you could possibly imagine.

Look, for example, what creativity can produce under added incentive—despite mood—when a nation goes to war. The genius is, of course, directed toward destructive as well as defensive measures, but the creativity must be called on to produce whether the creator feels like it or not.

Take free-lance writers. They have no boss other than themselves. They can work when they feel like it—if they feel like it. But most writers set definite hours for their daily work, just as if they were going to an office.

Does their creativity suffer? No. No writers can truthfully say that they write any worse when they set themselves down to writing than if they just write when the mood moves them.

The need for survival, the need to earn, is usually the motivating power. You now understand all about the incentive that creates your motive, from your reading of the chapter on Your Memory Motive.

The writer, the inventor, the artist . . . all can work as well when they have to as when they want to. As often as not, in fact, *having* to work produces a better product.

BEING A MOOD SLAVE IS A LOSS OF TIME _____

All you accomplish by being a slave to your moods is the loss of time. But time is too valuable to lose. Time is too fleeting. It seems that the only thing faster than the way Todays become Yesterdays is the way Tomorrows become Todays.

Worst of all, by giving in to your moods you rapidly develop the habit of withdrawing from the very work that would increase your power to remember successfully.

Like all bad habits, the habit of withdrawing from your prescribed work is a hindrance to the complete accomplishment of bettering your power to remember successfully.

You now come to the second stage of developing a pattern of work that will bring you to the hundred-per-cent level rapidly.

Don't develop bad habits in remembering; develop good habits.

It's as simple as that. The bad habits of remembering are those of giving in to your moods. The bad habits are the creating of, listening to, and believing your own excuses.

How many excuses can you make to avoid accomplishing the power to remember successfully?

"I just lack the confidence in myself."
"Perhaps it's because I'm too easily distracted."
"Oh, I'm just absent-minded."
"Try to remember? That makes me tired."
"I can't concentrate on anything for long enough."
"Maybe it's because I'm not really interested enough."
"My mind wanders on to other things all the time."
"I never could remember anything."
"I'm just not in the mood."

And I'll wager you can add another dozen or more. These are the bad habits, the habits into which anyone can slip all too easily, the habits that will defeat your purpose—the development of your power to remember successfully.

MAKE A SCHEDULE FOR YOURSELF _____

The minute your alibi-offering brain serves up one of these excuses, look yourself straight in the eye and say: "I must not allow a bad habit to control me. I must control my habits!"

Having recognized the alibi, you now have to counter its plan by continuing your work. Since it makes no difference whether you are in the mood, or whether you would rather do something else at the moment, or whether you think you are not interested just now—set aside a definite time in every day to work on making your remembering power successful.

Use for your planning the daily schedule shown on the next page.

First fill in the hours of each day that are definitely used for your work at employment or home.

Next take one free hour early in every day—preferably the same one, but not necessarily—and write into it the word:

REMEMBER

This is the key word in developing the good habit that is going to bring you to complete mastery of your memory. This is the vital word in the power to remember successfully.

In that hour of every day that you have set aside to "remember," read a new chapter of this book.

Spend the full hour reading, digesting, understanding, learning the rules, and rereading.

Now find one free hour late in every day—preferably the last hour before you retire—and write into it the word:

REFRESH

This is the second key word in developing the habit of re-membering.

At that hour every day, just before you fall asleep, reread the chapter that you read and digested earlier in the day. Reread it slowly and carefully. Then put the book down and go to sleep.

This is the good-habit plan that will enable you to make the maximum use of your time and energy. This is the good-habit plan that will help you banish the alibis and bring you quickly to the full use of your power to remember successfully.

Follow this plan daily. Don't think that you cannot.

You can and will if you are serious in your desire to improve your memory.

Trying to believe that you can't follow a plan of this sort is a notion destructive to your memory.

DAILY SCHEDULE

	SUNDAY	MONDAY	TUESDAY	WEDNESDAY	THURSDAY	FRIDAY	SATURDAY
8 A.M.							
9 "							
10 "							
11 "							
NOON							
1 P.M.							
2 "							
3 "							
4 "							
5 "							
6 "							
7 "							
8 "							
9 "							
10 "							
11 "							

PRECONCEIVED IDEAS ARE DESTRUCTIVE _____

One of the most overburdening drawbacks to developing your power to remember is that of preconceived feelings about the very things you are trying to remember.

A commonly used experiment to show how preconception can affect one's ability to remember is that of showing people a photograph relating to something about which they hold strong opinions.

For instance, during the Vietnam War, a group of officer candidates were shown a photograph depicting a commando action. The photograph showed an American soldier, knife upraised in one hand, attacking a North Vietnamese rifleman.

After a second or two the picture was taken away and the officer candidates were asked to tell what they saw.

The results were no different from those always achieved in this type of test. Most of the young men recalled seeing the North Vietnamese as the aggressor and the American soldier unaware of the attack.

The preconceived notion that the North Vietnamese were the enemy and therefore not to be trusted interfered with the memories of these officer candidates.

Another experiment conducted by psychologists involved a group of people whose political ideas were known. Half the group chosen were pro-Republican and the other half pro-Democratic. The group were brought together and given a ten-minute speech on national affairs.

Content of the speech was carefully prepared so that half of it was anti-Democratic and half of it pro-Democratic. The group were told that they were being tested for memory. But they were not questioned on the speech until twenty-one days later.

At that time the preconceived ideas of the group's members showed clearly in the answers they gave to questions about the contents of the speech. Those of the group who were pro-Republican remembered most of the anti-Democratic segments of the speech. Those who were pro-Democratic remembered those portions of the speech that harmonized with their notions.

What you *think* you will see or hear, or what you *prefer* to see or hear, most often determines what you will remember having seen or heard. Sometimes the memory will be of something you did not see or hear at all. This is a pitfall that you must avoid.

Similarly you must realize that you can follow a daily plan of successfully improving your powers to remember. You are now aware that your preconceptions can play tricks on you so you must determine never to become involved in a situation where your memory will play tricks on you by remembering things you have never seen or heard.

YOUR DAILY PLAN

The daily plan that you have established to aid you in increasing your power to remember is the exact plan that you will use later in increasing your memory-efficiency and putting it to use for whatever purpose, or purposes, you require it.

Whenever you use the daily plan of remembering and refreshing—to give you memory-efficiency in the task or tasks you have set for yourself after you have learned all the secrets of improving your memory successfully—turn back to your daily schedule and put to use the same hours of remembering and refreshing.

These are the hours that are important to you.

Use them, and use them well.

In using them, however, you have to avoid another pitfall. That is the barrier of discouragement.

DON'T BECOME DISCOURAGED _____

There is no "yardstick" that you can set—or that any so-called expert can set—that will determine just how much you will remember in any one day.

For some time you will find that you are acquiring new knowledge with great rapidity. Your memory-efficiency will seem to be working overtime for you. But, all of a sudden, you will find that you will have reached a point of levelling-off.

In fact, it will seem at times that you have suddenly ceased to remember any more. You will doubt your own powers to remember successfully. You will feel that you lack memory-efficiency.

This is not so.

This is only a time that occurs with everyone which I call the *Dead-Level of Learning.* No one can foretell when it will come. But it will come at some time after you have set out on a task of learning new material.

It may prove a little discouraging to you to find that you have suddenly levelled off. *Don't be discouraged, though; it is a very normal period.* It is like the organic process that people on weight-reducing diets discover when they find they have stopped losing weight short of their set goal.

At the start of any project you will utilize your power of remembering. You will find the path "greased" with the preliminary knowledge you have of the subject. This "greasing" facilitates those early days and you find yourself skimming along like a youngster on a toboggan coasting down a freshly snow-covered hill.

This preliminary knowledge is, however, limited. Suddenly you find yourself trying to remember facts, or words, or numbers, or whatever, that you never have seen before.

The remembering process seems to slow up. In fact, it seems to come to a dead stop. It has reached a plateau. But just because it is on this dead-level doesn't mean that it has stopped. The child's toboggan still moves along the plateau until it hits the next slope.

Your power to remember is moving along the dead-level until it reaches the next upward climb that your memory will take.

This dead-level of learning is not much different from the action of shifting gears in an automobile. Moving from gear to gear, you temporarily are in neutral. The automobile is moving, but momentarily not gaining speed—not until you place it into a higher gear.

This dead-level can be a discouraging time—but only if you allow it to be. If you do allow discouragement to creep into your road to successful remembering, you have acquired a far worse habit than the ones you have already discarded.

If you are going to learn to use your power to remember successfully, you must realize that learning to remember efficiently is a process that takes place in stages.

> *1. You will quickly find that with your initial interest and preliminary knowledge of the subject you start sailing smoothly and simply.*
> *2. Suddenly, as though you had taken your foot off the accelerator in your car, you will find yourself coasting—in fact, it will appear as if you are losing ground although you are not.*
> *3. Just as suddenly the Dead-Level of Learning will be passed; you will be sailing ahead again as soon as your processes of retention click into high gear.*
> *4. You will find yourself successful in making the fullest use of your power to remember.*

Does it sound easy? It is! In fact it is even easier than it sounds.

MORE EXCUSES—BRAIN FATIGUE

"But I get tired of learning. I have to stop and rest because my brain gets weary!"

That's the *Excuse Extreme!*

The other alibis—up to this point—have at least had the most infinitesimal basis in truth: truth, that is, that sadly exposes the alibier as being a procrastinator.

But this is an alibi that is no alibi at all.

There is no such thing as your brain getting weary. I've often heard people speak of "brain fatigue." *It does not exist.*

Your brain is not like a muscle. Long and concentrated mental effort cannot produce tiredness in the wonderful machine inside your skull. If it seems to you that you are tired after a long period of mental work, the fatigue is located in other parts of the body.

Think back to the last time you suddenly became tired after a lengthy mental chore. What parts of you were tired? Your eyes most likely, since they were used constantly and the muscles became strained. Your neck and back muscles, too, undoubtedly told a tale of muscular strain.

But your brain? It was as fresh the minute you stopped your project as the minute you started it.

One experiment showed that after doing the same mental task for twelve hours without a break, a young woman was able to perform the mental function with only a slight decrease in efficiency.

The experiment called for the multiplication of a series of two four-digit numbers, one after the other, as rapidly as possible—all in the young woman's head. She went on doing this without a stop for the twelve hours.

Her speed and accuracy were measured all the way through; these showed an infinitesimal decrease in efficiency. But she stopped at the end of that time—owing to sheer bodily fatigue and hunger.

What may seem to you to be mental fatigue is often only boredom. Most often, if the mental task you have set for yourself is comparatively difficult, you start to be torn between a desire to continue and to stop.

As a result of experiments in this field it has been discovered that fatigue is not the result of such work. Most often, said inattention and your inability to ignore a distracting thought are responsible.

In making use of your daily schedule to improve your power of remembering successfully, try to select a time in the day when you know you are most receptive to retaining the things you want to remember.

Your "learning efficiency" differs at various times of the day.

DETERMINE THE BEST MEMORY HOURS

Psychological studies indicate that most people are best able to use their memory-efficiency early in the day. In some cases it has been found that immediately upon awakening some persons have the highest peak of retention powers. In other cases an hour or two after awakening is best.

You have to decide, from experience, when you are best able to use your powers of remembering. That will be the key by which you determine which hour in every day is the one for which you will write **REMEMBER** in your daily chart.

By the same token, determine which hour in the evening is going to be the hour for **REFRESH.** Several studies have indicated that the memory-efficiency picks up between the hours of 8 P.M. and 10 P.M. This may be so in your case. Again, only experience will tell. But, once you have determined when you can best **REFRESH,** enter that hour on your daily chart and use it for your daily period of increasing your power to remember successfully.

Finally, the best method of preventing yourself from becoming a Mood Slave is by not allowing yourself to fall into the bad habit of relaxing while doing your daily stint of remembering.

Relaxation is the greatest ally of Mood Slavery. Sitting in a too-comfortable chair; reading in a prone position; any of these or similar conditions are going to set stumbling blocks in the path of your power to remember successfully.

Sit in a comfortable, but hard, chair for maximum efficiency. Don't allow yourself to get too comfortable for the hour you have set aside to improve your memory.

In a series of experiments, persons who were allowed to sit relaxed while doing mental tasks and then were set to performing similar tasks under conditions of some physical tension were found to have ten per cent greater efficiency in the uncomfortable positions than in the relaxed positions.

EIGHT STEPS TO SUCCESS

Remember:

> *Master your moods—you must not be a Mood Slave!*
>
> *Do it today—you must not procrastinate!*
>
> *Finish what you set out to do—you must not become sidetracked!*
>
> *Prepare a daily schedule—you must not work in hit-or-miss fashion!*

Continue to work through the Dead-Level stage—you must not become discouraged!

Your brain never will tire—you must not cater to the idea of brain fatigue!

Find your peak hour of efficiency—you must not try to use your memory-efficiency at the weakest time for your retentive powers!

Muscle tension aids your memory-efficiency—you must not work in a relaxed position!

Using this simple plan, you will increase by another step your power to remember successfully.

MEMORY METER

100%
90%
80%
70%
60%
50%
40%
30% Mood Mastery
20% Memory Motive
10% Normal Usage

5

MAKE IT MEANINGFUL

*The more intelligible a thing is, the more easily
is it retained in the memory.*
Spinoza: *Tractatus de Intellectus Emendatione.*

The more the meaning, the more the memory.

No matter what it is you have to remember, if it has meaning to you you can retain it easily and quickly.

The ardent golfer was once reminded by his wife not to forget the date of their wedding anniversary.

"Do you think I'd forget that day," the golfer retorted. "Why that was the day I sank a sixty-foot putt."

By giving something meaning for yourself, you cannot help but remember it.

Rote—much as you like to think it can—will not give you the degree of memory-efficiency you want with little effort.

Photographic memory—much as you have heard of it—does not exist; experiment proves this. But we will discuss this in a later chapter.

You can only use your power to remember successfully—and easily—by giving things meaning. The greater the meaning, the easier it is to remember.

"How can a lengthy number have meaning?"

"How can I put meaning into a shopping list?"

"How can I find meaning in a series of telephone numbers I have to remember?"

60

"How do I get meaning out of an order-code list?"

The list of questions could go on and on. I'm sure you have thought of at least one question you would like to ask about "making it meaningful."

EVERYTHING CAN HAVE MEANING

The answer to all the questions is: *You can give meaning to anything that you have to remember.*

Is it the serial number of a piece of machinery? Scrutinize the number carefully to see if it breaks down into components you already know. Perhaps it has an arithmetic or algebraic progression such as the serial number of a typewriter I once used: 235812. I remembered that number by adding one to 2, two to the resulting 3, three to the resulting five, and finally four to the resulting 8 which gave me $2 (+1) = 3 (+2) = 5 (+3) = 8 (+4) = 12$.

A friend remembered a long automobile license number because he discovered it broke down to his address followed by his street number and followed by his apartment number. He lived at 3332 East 99th Street, apartment 16; his license plate was 333-29-916.

Shopping lists prove even simpler to give meaning to. Suppose the list consists of shoes, gloves, umbrella, a card table, and a cake-serving fork. A simple readjustment will make your list meaningful in a counting sense:

umbrella = one (a single stick)

shoes = two (pair)

cake serving fork = three (it usually has three tynes)

card table = four (legs)

gloves = five (fingers)

Perhaps it is a grocery list comprising milk, apples, flour, eggs, and bread. Here, too, there is an easy readjustment alphabetically:

Apples - A
Bread - B
Milk - C (cow)
Flour - D (dough)
Eggs - E

Or you can readjust a shopping list in another fashion. Let us say you are going to buy tea, lettuce, eggs, apples, and pears. Readjust the list in this fashion:

Pears
Lettuce
Apples
Tea
Eggs

Then all you have to remember is the word PLATE, comprising the initial letters of the items you need.

EVEN TELEPHONE NUMBERS HAVE MEANING

What about telephone numbers? Can they be made meaningful?
Often numbers will lend themselves to easy meaningful memory. You would have no difficulty with the following numbers:
2244 (which means 2 + 2 = 4, yes 4 is correct).
3618 (which means 3 × 6 = 18).
2468 (which is counting by twos).
2173 (which means 21 ÷ 7 = 3).
Such combinations are easily made meaningful.
Actually some people remember telephone numbers only by the meaning they have attributed to them. They claim they could not remember them otherwise.

More difficult numbers can be made meaningful in this way: 467-8323 can be recalled with the word instead, which is made up of the initials on the dial phone that you get for that number. Here it is easier to use the coincident letters than to make sense of the numerals.

If you can't make a word of a number, make a pronounce-able syllable or syllables. For instance: 274-7428 might make CRIPHAT; or 836-2397 might make TENBEYS.

An order-code list can be made just as meaningful in just as simple a way.

For instance let us say that you are a book salesman. Your publisher uses a five-number code for all his books. These are rememberable in the same way as telephone numbers. You use the title of the book, or a key word in the title if it is a long one, to repre-sent the first two letters of the word you will make.

For example, let us say that there is a book called *Plumbing Made Easy,* and its code number is 28-328. This, transferred using the numbers on the telephone dial, could be PLATEAU—using PL for *Plumbing.* Or if a book titled *How to Catch Fish* had the number 36-497, this would be FIDOHYP—using FI for the key word *Fish.*

Using the letter of the alphabet that keys to the corres-ponding number is another system that can be used here. By transliterating A for 1, B for 2, C for 3, and so forth, a code number 017/254 becomes JAGBED.

If there is no other way to make numbers meaningful, try grouping them into rhythmic divisions. In this way 954618922 might become 954/618/922 in rhythm.

LETTER CODES ARE ADAPTABLE

A dress manufacturer I was told about uses a two-letter code for his styles. His salespeople found that they were always able to think of the initials used in the code as the initials of slogans, items, or real or imaginary people. So the dress-fashion code was transcribed and thought of in this manner:

> *BD—Baby Doll*
> *BR—Babe Ruth*
> *BO—Lifebuoy*
> *BP—Be Prepared*

These are the kind of things that you should avoid remembering by rote. While rote learning may give you the feeling that what you are trying to remember will be retained more quickly, it will also leave you more quickly.

Teachers tell the story of a little boy who had a great deal of difficulty with the past tense of the verb *to go.* He invariably used *went* when he should have used *gone.* Finally, his teacher became exasperated. She had him stay after school one day and write on the blackboard one hundred times:

"I have gone."

The boy, discouraged and unhappy at not being able to join his classmates at play, stayed and performed his chore. When he had completed it, his teacher was not in the room. Unwilling to await her return and most anxious to get outside to play, he appended a note to the "lines."

"I have finished, so I have went."

The rote writing had had no meaning to the youth other than being a punishment.

If you are to remember anything, it must have meaning to you.

PROOF THAT MEANING MAKES IT EASIER

A familiar psychological experiment is illustrated by these three groups of ten words. Read the lists carefully, one at a time, then close the book and try to write them in order on a piece of paper.

List A

1. THIS
2. SMALL
3. BOY
4. RAN
5. ALL
6. THE
7. WAY
8. TO
9. HIS
10. HOME

Now that you have written this list down as you remembered it, check to see how close you came to the original.

Read the second list, and try to write it on a piece of paper after you close the book.

List B

1. GIRL
2. PLAY
3. DOLL
4. DRESS
5. SHOES
6. SOCKS
7. HAT
8. CARRIAGE
9. WHEEL
10. AXLE

How did you fare on this list?

Now try the third list and see how many of the words you can remember in the order they are given.

List C

1. CAR
2. BOOK
3. SKY
4. FOOD
5. WORK
6. TREE
7. HELP
8. CHAIR
9. PEBBLE
10. CAN

Having written down the third list, let us compare the results of the three.

WHEN THERE'S MEANING, THERE'S UNDERSTANDING _____

You probably were able to remember the first list almost entirely in its correct order. Why? Because it made sense. It is a complete sentence.

The second list probably presented a little more of a problem. Perhaps you were able to recall six or more words in their correct order.

But the third list was the most difficult. It is a jumble of meaningless words. Those words you did remember probably were not in the order given.

The first list of words is a cohesive group. It has meaning to you. You can understand it. You conjured up a mental picture of the action and therefore had little difficulty in recalling the entire sentence.

There is some related meaning in the second group of words. You were able, therefore, to get some sort of a picture that would help you relate the words to meaning and therefore help you remember them.

The last group, completely unrelated, made a jumble in your mind. It had no meaning at first glance and was therefore difficult to remember.

The meaningfulness of the first group of words is obvious and complete.

If it were actually necessary for you to remember the second group of words, you could add meaning to complete your mental picture; then the words would be easily recalled.

Meaning for the second group is fairly easy to achieve: a **girl play**ing with her **doll** is **dress**ing it with **shoes, socks** and a **hat,** and placing it in a **carriage** with a **wheel** missing from one **axle.**

With this meaning attached, you can more easily remember most of the words on the first try and get them in the right order. Go back and read list *B* again and now write the ten words of this list in order.

Did you do better this time? Undoubtedly.

Now, what can be done to give meaning to list *C* with which you had the greatest difficulty in the previous test? Is it possible to make a cohesive sentence out of the words as you did with the second group? No; a meaningful sentence seems out of the question. Then why not try to give the words meaning in groups of two, thus:

Car-book; sky-food; work-tree; help-chair; pebble-can.

Read that last grouping again. Now close the book and see how many of the words you can remember in sequence.

Did you do better this time? Undoubtedly.

TRY ADDING RHYTHM _____

You can use the system of adding meaning or rhythm—which was explained in recalling numbers—to remember a group of nonsense syllables. Syllables with no meaning are difficult to remember. For example, here are two lists of syllables. Look first at list *D* and write down the time you started to look at it.

Then read it until you have it completely memorized. When that is done, write down the time you were finished.

Time started _____

List D

  1. WAX
  2. COW
  3. EGG
  4. RUN
  5. JAM
  6. KILL
  7. TRAP
  8. SLAM
  9. HARD
10. EARN

Time finished memorizing _____

Now try the same thing with list *E.*

Time started _____

List E

  1. TUK
  2. JOL
  3. ZAM
  4. YOT
  5. BUK
  6. GRAN
  7. BRYD
  8. SNOP
  9. KLUG
10. BLEM

Time finished memorizing _____

Which list took longer to remember? Undoubtedly list *E* required longer—perhaps as much as ten times longer—to remember than list *D.*

Now, for the sake of experiment, go back to list *E* and see if you can't give some meaning to each of the nonsense syllables. Let's start at the top of the list with a few examples and then you fill in the rest.

List E

1. TUK — *tuck*
2. JOL — *jolly*
3. ZAM — *slam*
4. YOT — _____
5. BUK — _____
6. GRAN — _____
7. BRYD — _____
8. SNOP — _____
9. KLUG — _____
10. BLEM — _____

Having given these nonsense syllables meaning, you can see how they now resemble list *D* more closely. Therefore, with meaning added to each syllable, list *E* could now be memorized as quickly as list *D.*

THE PRINCIPLE OF ASSOCIATION _____

The meanings you have given to the nonsense syllables in list *E* show you the value of the principal means of "making it meaningful"—*association.*

What do we mean by association?

Simply that you must *associate* an idea or word that has meaning to you with the idea or word that you wish to remember.

How can you make association apply to remembering?

There is no one answer; there are many ways. The secret is to select the way that is easiest for you, the way that will lend itself most directly to what you want to remember.

One of the prime methods of associating in order to use your power of remembering successfully is by employing the *Mental Hook Method.*

"Memory experts" who give courses by mail order or in the lecture hall, insist that their students memorize a list of several hundred words. This is their association list. The students are to use this lengthy list to help them associate things for improved memory.

What a lot of unnecessary work!

In the first place, if you are to memorize a list of several hundred words, the work and energy expended is fantastic. You could much more easily remember all the things you wanted to than learn the association list.

Secondly, after memorizing this massive list, you then have to memorize the association with those words of all the things you are trying to remember. Does it sound confusing? It is; and it increases the work of memorizing another ten-fold.

DISCOVERING YOUR MENTAL HOOKS

With the Mental Hook Method, you use only ten words. This method is designed purely to help you remember short lists of things. It is of of no value in remembering more complicated material; association lists in such cases are only a confusion. But we will look at the secrets of remembering complicated material in a later chapter.

The Mental Hooks are simple words. Ten simple words that you cannot forget. And they don't have to be learned the hard way.

Let us have a look at your Mental Hook list and see how it has been derived. This will give you a mental picture of each word in the list and an understanding of why the list has been arranged in the order given.

Mental Hook List

1. **Me**—*1 stands for one person: me. Therefore you have a simple connection for your first word.*

2. **Shoe**—*2 is a pair; 2 rhymes with shoe and shoes come in pairs.*

3. **Kittens**—*3 is the number of kittens there were in the childhood rhyme about the kittens that lost their mittens.*

4. **Table**—*4 represents the number of legs on a table.*

5. **Fingers**—*5 is the number of fingers you have on each hand.*

6. **Sticks**—*6, as you will recall from childhood days, rhymes with the word sticks: "five, six, pick up sticks."*

7. **Dice**—7 *is a lucky roll in dice.*

8. **Gate**—8 *is the number of bars on the old front gate, with which it rhymes.*

9. **Baseball**—9 *is the number of men on a baseball team.*

10. **Indians**—10 *little Indians, and then there were . . . remember?*

Now let us look at the list as it stands alone:

1. *Me*
2. *Shoe*
3. *Kittens*
4. *Table*
5. *Fingers*
6. *Sticks*
7. *Dice*
8. *Gate*
9. *Baseball*
10. *Indians*

Read it over once again. Now close the book and recite the list—in order—out loud. Wasn't that easy? Why? Because the associations you have developed with the list bring to mind very easily what the list is.

PUTTING THE MENTAL HOOKS TO USE _____

"Very simple," you say. "So I can remember the list: me, shoe, kittens, table, fingers, sticks, dice, gate, baseball, Indians. But what do I do with it?"

Well, it is even more simple to put it to use than it is to remember the list!

Your Mental Hook list will help you catch all those elusive fish that swim out of reach in your memory. Is it appointments you can't remember? Is it a list of points for a speech you are to make at a sales meeting? Perhaps a list of addresses you have to visit tomorrow afternoon?

There are hundreds of tasks that the Mental Hook list is going to help you successfully perform by helping you remember with efficiency.

Let us suppose it is a list of appointments. How will the Mental Hook list help?

Let's look at your appointment book for tomorrow:

9 A.M.	
10 A.M.	Barber
11 A.M.	
NOON	
1 P.M.	Eye Doctor
2 P.M.	Travel agent — pick up vacation ticket
3 P.M.	
4 P.M.	Cocktails—Mr. O'Hare
5 P.M.	

You are not going to carry your appointment book with you; and you are not going to have a chance to check it again after you leave for the day.

Are you going to remember all your appointments? Certainly. Your handy Mental Hook list—which you now remember accurately—will assure you of remembering them.

Here's how:

*Ten o'clock—10—Indians—**you see Indians doing a war dance and scalping a man**—scalping—hair—barber.*
*One o'clock—1—me—**me is no one else than I, and I have eyes**—eyes—eye doctor.*
*Two o'clock—2—shoe—**you see yourself, with shoes brighly polished, walking up the gangplank of a cruise ship**—cruise—travel agency.*
*Four o'clock—4—table—**you see a table with people sitting around in chairs**—chair—O'Hare.*

IT WORKS BACKWARD TOO

Or perhaps your remember where you have to go, but can't think of what time you have your appointments.

Let's try it that way and see how the Mental Hooks work for you.

> *Barber—**barber cuts off hair—so do Indians on the war-**
> **path**—Indians?—That's 10: So, 10 a.m.*
> *Eye doctor—**eye doctor is going to help me**—me?—That's*
> *1: So 1 p.m.*
> *Travel agency—**travel means going places, much of it***
> ***done by foot—foot wears a shoe**—shoe? That's 2: So, 2*
> *p.m.*
> *Mr. O'Hare—**Mr. O'Hare is to be met for cocktails; he'll be***
> ***sitting in the lounge at a table**—table? That's 4: So 4 p.m.*

It's utterly impossible to get your appointments mixed up. You won't keep Mr. O'Hare waiting; nor will you cause the eye doctor annoyance by turning up at 2 P.M. when he has another patient.

Suppose you have to make a speech tomorrow. And you want to talk without notes. How can your Mental Hooks help?

Let us say you are speaking on U.S. foreign policy. Your speech is divided into five sections:

I. History of foreign relations in the United States
II. Foreign policy under Democratic administrations
III. Foreign policy under Republican administrations
IV. Current foreign policy
V. The future of American foreign relations

You now have to relate these points to your Mental Hook list so that you will not skip a vital segment of your speech and so that you will give it in its proper order. Let us study the speech point by point in relation to the Mental Hook list.

> *First point: 1—me—**you think of yourself reading up on***
> ***the background of your subject in a heavy history***
> ***book**—history.*
> *Second point: 2—shoe—**you think of a shoe with a hole in***
> ***it, the campaign tag of two-time Democratic candidate***
> ***Adlai Stevenson**—Democrats.*

*Third point: 3—kittens—**you see some kittens playing on the carpet as you vacuum it; vacuum cleaner: Hoover**—Republicans.*
*Fourth point: 4—table—**you see a group of legislators sitting around a table thrashing out an important issue; it's happening right now**—current.*
*Fifth point: 5—fingers—**you see yourself pointing off into the distance**—future.*

OTHER TRICKS TO HELP YOU REMEMBER

What are other tricks that you can use to help yourself remember?

There are a whole list of memory tricks known as *mnemonic devices.* These are Mental Hooks that are well known to you in many forms. These mnemonic devices, as the psychologists call them, are only gimmicks designed to aid the memory.

For instance, how often have you used the little rhyme that you must have learned in school days, starting: *"Thirty days hath September . . . "?*

Or you must have used another rhyme that you learned in school:

"'I' before 'e'
Except after 'c'
Or when sounded like 'a'
As in neighbor and weigh."

That one is an easy way to help you with those catchy words that use the "i," "e" combination.

And the "Thirty days hath September" rhyme is a wonderful way to remember how many days there are in each month. European children learn another mnemonic trick to remember how many days there are in the months. They are told to place their hands in front of them, clench their fists, then use the knuckles showing uppermost at the end of the fingers and the valleys between them as the months. In that way the knuckle of the little finger on your left hand is January (raised and therefore a long month—31 days), the valley beside it is February (a short month), the knuckle of the ring finger is March (a long month), and so forth. Where the hands come together, the knuckles of both index fingers make July and August, the only two months next to each other that have an equal number of days.

There are countless mnemonic devices that people use daily to recall things that they feel they may not otherwise be able to remember at the moment they want them.

A guide in one of this country's vast underground caverns once told me that the only way he could remember the difference between stalagmites and stalactites—those beautiful stone pillars found in all underground caverns—was this:

"I always think of the end of the second syllable," he said during a tour through the caverns. "The second syllable of stalagmites ends with a 'G'—so I think of 'stalag'—G—ground. They are the ones that rise from the ground.

"The second syllable of stalactites ends with a 'C'—so I think: 'stalac?'—C—ceiling. They are the ones that drop from the ceiling."

Have you ever noticed the signs that many restaurants have during the months from September to April that say: "Oysters R in season." That's a Mental Hook type of device to remind you that every month that is spelled with an 'r' in it is a month in which oysters are available.

EVEN MUSIC USES MNEMONICS

I'm sure that your music teacher taught you a number of such Mental Hook tricks to recall various essentials. The first such mnemonic device most music teachers use is for the spaces in the treble clef, which spell "face" thus:

For the lines in the same clef, the little sentence *"Every Good Boy Deserves Favors"* is used to remember the initial letters E G B D F, which transferred to the clef make it

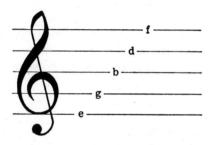

If you have ever played a ukulele you will recall how, to tune the instrument, you sang a little tune to yourself which you never forgot because it was set to the words: "My Dog Has Fleas."

There are countless other such Mental Hooks in common usage. That means that there are many ways in which you can use mnemonic devices and make them work for you.

A brilliant pianist I knew of used music to help him with telephone numbers. He transcribed the numbers mentally into the scale and then sang them to himself every time he wanted to dial them.

A few pages back, I showed you how to remember telephone numbers by making words out of them. This is a mnemonic device that is often used. One woman I know does this to all telephone numbers. She once told me some of the words or names she remembers together with the people the numbers belong to, and her system went something like this:

Ms. Silver's phone number is 637-2879. The phone number has been transcribed as "mercury," so that in my friend's mind the association is "Silver—mercury."

Ms. Mann's number is 364-5474, which my friend transcribed into "English" so that the association in her mind is "English—Mann."

TRICKS FOR SPELLING AND HISTORY _____

A young secretary I know has difficulty remembering the spelling of certain words; so she worked out a series of Mental Hooks for herself to give her aid when she needs it. For instance, she told me, she is never quite sure whether you spell it "expense" or "expence." She solved it by thinking that expense involves money and now she always sees the word in her mind's eye as "expen$e."

A history teacher once indicated to me that she helped all her classes with little mnemonic tricks. Some of these were:

*F*ranklin *P*ierce was the *F*ourteenth *P*resident of the United States. The initials in each case helped. Or to remember Lincoln's first vice-president she would write the president's name as

AbraHAM LINcoln

and thus the name of Hamlin appeared.

Near the beginning of the chapter I used another mnemonic device to help you with shopping lists. By making a word, or a pronounceable syllable, out of the initial letters of the items on the list, you have a ready Memory Hook to take out with you on your shopping trip.

For instance:

If you are going to the department store to get shoes, stockings, handkerchiefs, andirons, and towels, write this list this way—

Shoes
Towels
Andirons
Stockings
Handkerchiefs

so that you remember the word "stash" as the Memory Hook for your list.

Or if you are going to the fruit store for apples, peaches, oranges, grapefruit, and bananas, write the list this way—

Peaches
Apples
Grapefruit
Oranges
Bananas

and remember the pronounceable syllables "pagob" as your Memory Hook.

The use of puns is another Mental Hook that you will find invaluable in remembering any number of things—especially names.

A teacher with whom I once worked used the Mental Hook pun to recall the names of all the students in her classes.

A young man named Henry Fowler she remembered because he played on the basketball team and had often been benched during games for excessive personal fouling—so it became "fouler" —Fowler in her mind. A girl named Sylvia Boeing was a violinist and in this teacher's Mental Hook method the pun of "bowing"— Boeing was an easy one.

Puns can be used in many ways and are an easy method of making Mental Hooks for yourself.

MAKING A MEMORY CHAIN

Another easy method of helping develop your power to remember is by connecting things you wish to remember with other things you already know.

This method of recall is the basis for certain courses that some universities now give. For instance, at Columbia University in New York a course in Civilization utilizes the idea of tying known material to material being learned. History, literature, geography, sociology and such subjects are made into a chain by periods so that an over-all picture is readily available in the mind's eye.

In this way, for instance, by recalling that Franklin Pierce was elected president of this country in 1852, you tie in such other facts as that being the year the Dogma of the Immaculate Conception of the Virgin Mary was adopted, Napoleon III was crowned Emperor of France, Daniel Webster failed to get his party's nomination as presidential candidate and later died, Roget published his famous *Thesaurus of English Words and Phrases,* and Harriet Beecher Stowe's *Uncle Tom's Cabin* was issued.

Association with things known has been used by many people to remember numbers of all sorts: addresses, phone numbers, order listings, catalogue lists, and such. Wherever possible they use historical dates to tie in with the number to be remembered. In this way Ms. Jones, on whom you may have to call for a donation to your favorite charity, might live at "Pearl Harbor Main Street" if her address is 1941 Main Street.

The order numbers of various styles of gloves sold in the store for which you are the buyer can become Independence (1776) Revolution (1775), Constitution (1787), Washington (1789), and the like.

MAKE IT VIVID!

Another simple way to help energize your power to remember is by the rule of vividness.

A vivid impression is far more easily remembered than a "run of the mill" impression. You well know that a startling occurrence is going to stick in your memory much more than an everyday happening. For instance, if on your way home one day after getting off the bus you passed a person walking down the street, and the next day you stumbled over a body lying on the street, which would you be more likely to recall?

Of course, you would always remember suddenly tripping over a body. But the simple occurrence of passing a person on the street would not be remembered more than a short time.

Many experiments have shown that a vivid item is immediately recalled. It can also later be recalled more easily, and can also be relearned more quickly if forgotten.

One experiment gave a group of persons two nine-syllable lists. In the first list all the syllables were printed in black letters on white paper. After it was discovered which syllable was most readily forgotten because of its position in the list, a second list was given to the group. On this list, the syllable in the position that was least rememberable on the first list was printed in red letters on a green background.

The vivid effect made that syllable the most easily learned and the most easily recalled.

If there is any way in which the things you desire to remember can be made to stand out vividly in your mind, use it. It is a guarantee that you will achieve the Fabulous Forty on your route to gaining the full power of remembering successfully.

IMPORTANT THINGS ARE VIVID THINGS

Things that are important to you can sometimes help make other things vivid in your own mind.

They tell a story about a visitor to New York who asked two teen-aged girls where the Empire State Building was.

Pointing down the street, one of the rock-happy girls said:

"You can't miss it. It's right across the street from the record shop!"

A friend of mine who always complained that her husband never noticed what she wore, set out to change the situation. This she accomplished by making her point a vivid one.

As they were about to go out one evening, her husband stopped her as she was stepping out of their home.

"Yikes, what have you got on?" he asked. "A nightie?"

"Yes. And now that you've noticed what I'm wearing," the woman said, "I'll go back and put on a dress."

A vivid impression once reminded the great violinist, Fritz Kreisler, of a concert date. He was walking along the street with a friend when they passed a fish store. Kreisler noticed the window display of codfish, mouths open and eyes staring, when he suddenly stopped and exclaimed:

"Heavens—that reminds me! I have to play at a concert tonight!"

The trick of vividness is the same Memory Hook that you used in creating certain silly associations when you wanted to remember your list of appointments or the points in your speech. Those ridiculous pictures that you conjured up were vivid ones and therefore remained in your memory with ease.

Any way in which you can bring out something vividly in your own mind is going to be a way to help you gain the next step in accomplishing a successful memory. The tricks of remembering are a valuable aid in acquiring the full power of your wonderful remembering machine—the brain.

Remember:

It must have meaning.

The more the meaning, the more the memory.

Make and use your Mental Hooks.

Learn to associate meaning to your Mental Hooks.

Utilize other mnemonic devices.

Meaning and Mental Hooks make for masterful memory.

MEMORY METER

100%	
90%	
80%	
70%	
60%	
50%	
40%	Mental Hooks
30%	Mood Mastery
20%	Memory Motive
10%	Normal Usage

6

GOALS YOU CAN GAIN QUICKLY

Is anything more important than goals? I can't imagine. They distract us from our smaller distractions, anxieties, and problems and magnetically pull us upward and upward. After all, the tension between "I got it" and the "I want it" is God's way of needling us to succeed.
Dr. Robert Schuller.

Everything you do has an end in view!

That end is the *goal.*

That end is the target at which you are aiming. It is the height to which you are reaching.

Knowing you have a goal, is the primary rule in increasing your power to remember successfully.

Recognizing what the goal is, is the second rule.

Getting to that goal, is the purpose of this book.

When you started to read this book, you were shown that you would be able to bring your memory-efficiency up through the ladder from its ten-per-cent usage to its fullest powers.

This means, therefore, that by reading this book you are striving for—and reaching—a goal: the goal of a successful memory. So it is that everything you wish to achieve—everything for which you seek to improve your power of remembering—must have a goal at its climax.

This is the basis of our primary rule of gaining your goal: *knowing you have a goal.*

WHAT IS YOUR GOAL? _____

Why are you reading this book? To successfully increase your power to remember.

This is your first goal. Once you have achieved it, what do you intend to do with it?

That is an answer, of course, which you must give yourself. But whatever your ultimate aim is in improving your memory-efficiency, once you have accomplished the improvement of your power to remember, you can accomplish many other goals you desire—simply.

I have no idea what goal you may have in mind, after you have finished reading this book and have increased your power to remember.

Perhaps you are taking your first trip to Europe and you want to learn the language of the country you are going to visit.

Perhaps you are taking a new job and want to remember all the regulations concerning it before you start your first day.

Maybe you have volunteered to help your service club in its drive for a particular project and you have been asked to speak to various small groups throughout the city. You want to perfect your power to remember so that you can speak on all the points to be covered and can answer any questions that are asked.

Perhaps, as I did, you want to go on a quiz show and wish to gather up all the information you think will be required to be a prize-winner.

It could be any of a thousand reasons.

It doesn't matter what the reason is. The only thing that matters is that you have a purpose—a *goal.*

You have to recognize exactly what that goal is—tangibly. Without that recognition, it is impossible to set out to reach it.

Is it the learning of French?

Is it the regulations of your new job?

Is it the information about a club project?

Is it the winning of a quiz show program?

With this concrete information in hand, you know where you are going.

THE PULLING POWER OF THE GOAL _____

All manner of experiments have shown that with a goal in sight it is easier to accomplish what you want to do. The closer you get to a goal, the greater is that goal's pulling power.

It is much like a magnet. The farther away a piece of metal is from a magnet, the less is the power to pull that metal to the magnet. The closer the metal is, the greater is the power of the magnet.

With any chore you set out to do, whether it is a physical or a mental one, it has been found invariably that the closer you are to the end of that chore the faster you work. Also, the closer you are to accomplishing what you set out to do, the less likely you are to make mistakes.

This is the pulling power of the goal. The closer you are to the goal you have set out to reach, the greater is your efficiency in performing the task that you must perform to reach the goal.

One experiment that psychologists tried involved a group of farm hands in a wheat field. All were competent workers with scythes.

The farm hands were divided into two groups and each group was set to working on opposite sides of a large wheat field. The only difference in the process was that on one side of the field red flags were set up every three feet.

Both groups started to reap the wheat at the same moment. But it was found that the group working on the side of the field marked with flags worked with greater speed. In addition, it was discovered, the closer the "flag" group came to each of the markers, the faster and more efficiently did they work.

The experiment was tried the next day with the groups reversed. This time the second group—now working with the flags—worked more quickly, as had the first group the day before.

The results of this experiment show clearly the pulling power of the goal.

MOVING CLOSER TO ACHIEVEMENT _____

There is a surging of exultation within you when you realize that you are nearing your goal. With almost unconscious reaction you seek to move closer to achievement.

This pulling power is observed in the way rats perform in a maze. It has been shown time and again that the rat is able to eliminate the dead-ends nearest the goal faster than it is able to eliminate those nearest the entrance to the maze.

In running the course of the maze, the rat shows an increase of speed as it comes closer to the goal. This increase in speed, or in efficiency, as one reaches the "end in sight," or the goal, is known as the *goal gradient.*

A common instance of how this *goal gradient* operates is seen in a crowd waiting in line outside a motion-picture theater. The line of people will stand quite quietly until approximately the time for the show-break.

As soon as it becomes apparent that the picture is about to end and that the crowd inside will depart, the people in the line start to edge closer to the entrance—even though they are not getting into the theater, nor are they going to enter any sooner.

It is the *goal gradient* at work. It is the realization that the goal is in sight. The end to be achieved is near. The surging forward is an unconscious reaction.

USING YOUR GOAL GRADIENT

Just how can you utilize the *goal gradient?*

What can be done with it to help you increase your power to remember?

You now understand that the *goal gradient* exists. You realize that each time you near a goal your efficiency increases and your power to reach your goal surges forward at a faster rate. Therefore you must set many intermediate goals for yourself along the path to accomplishment and achievement.

You have had from the start an over-all goal in whatever you set out to accomplish.

But now you must set more immediately attainable goals to speed you on your way.

Let us use the example of this book and what it will do for you.

The accomplishment of memory-efficiency, the power to remember successfully, is your over-all goal.

Are you taking the entire text of this book and trying to swallow it all in one chunk?

No! You are reading and absorbing this book chapter by chapter. Better still, you probably are reading and absorbing each chapter section by section.

You are unconsciously using the rule of intermediate goals.

You have set for yourself daily goals in absorbing this book. You are accomplishing your goals and you are rapidly reaching the aim of a successful memory.

You are doing it by the very method you must use in every approach you take toward utilizing your wonderful power to remember.

ELIMINATING THE DEAD-LEVELS

By setting intermediate goals you eliminate the dead-level area we discussed in Chapter 4 Mastering Your Moods. You have a small section of the "whole" to accomplish. You can accomplish this small section easily. Every time you near an intermediate goal, you increase your power, your efficiency, and your speed.

In a short time all your intermediate goals are passed and your major goal—the aim that you have set out to accomplish—is in sight. This nearing of the major goal is the greatest incentive to increased power, efficiency, and speed.

It is the ultimate in using the *goal gradient* for your greater benefit.

So you see that your goal—whatever it is—has a pulling power. It is a pulling power that you must use. It is just like the magnet I described, pulling you to achievement.

If you are going to learn French, for example, the setting of that long-range goal may be discouraging to you just in the planning. But by utilizing intermediate goals you can find yourself swinging down the lane to perfection in the language in jig time.

Suppose you set for yourself a series of intermediate goals of learning ten new nouns a day. As each list nears completion, you will find that you are remembering with greater speed and skill and are making use of the newly acquired language with increased efficiency.

As each list disappears behind you, and succeeding lists of verbs, adjectives, and adverbs do likewise, you will find that learning the language is not a chore, is not tedious, has no dead-level periods, and is accomplished in a manner that will surprise you in retrospect.

EACH GOAL INCREASES EFFICIENCY _____

The same applies to any other task: the learning of the regulations for a new job, the acquiring of facts for your speaking tour, the gathering of information for your quiz-show appearance, or any other task you have set.

You have tangible goals all along the way. You get the increase in efficiency as you come closer to each goal. And your efficiency increases with each goal reached so that as you move from intermediate step to intermediate step you speed up noticeably.

One Psychologist, Robert S. Woodworth, used the example of the person trying to jump into the air. Just making a leap into the air will never bring you as high as leaping over a barrier set between two poles. And as the barrier is moved higher—each an intermediate goal—you find that you can succeed in leaping higher and higher.

The same principle—having something to work against—applies in the running of races where time records are sought. When distance runners try to shatter existing records, they will "run against the clock," as they say, and use as intermediate goals a number of opponents running short distances at sprint speeds to pace them.

An experiment that clearly shows how working "against" a barrier, or "toward" an intermediate goal, is an added incentive, is the one in which several persons are given a certain test.

Before the test starts, the group is told that another group has just finished the test. The results of this mythical group are then read to the group being tested and the test is started. The group—competing with a fictitious group—will invariably do better than a group that simply takes the test without the incentive of competition.

The first group has a goal to work toward.

The second group has no goal to work toward.

HARNESSING YOUR GOAL POWER _____

Set a goal for yourself. Establish intermediate goals along the way. Use the goal gradient. Allow the pulling power of the goal to bring you to your desired aim with success, speed, and ease.

This is the power that you can harness. This is the power that you must harness to your advantage.

"Is there any set and prescribed way of dividing my work aim into intermediate goals?"

That is a question that has often been asked of me and quite frankly I must answer:

No—no one can honestly tell you what your own intermediate goals should be; just as no one can tell you what your aims in life must be.

Decide for yourself what the best period of work or the greatest amount of work is for you in any given day. Then divide that period or amount into workable portions.

For instance, if you find that you can work best for one hour in the morning, then find out just how you work in that hour. Do you find yourself working in ten-minute spurts? Or do you perhaps find twelve or fifteen minutes is more advantageous to you?

In doing work such as developing your power to remember, as you are doing now, do you find it best to read one chapter at a time?

In that one chapter, do you find the greatest interest and efficiency of absorption in sections embodying one topic? Or two topics? Or more?

> *Utilize this information to help you adopt a plan of setting a goal for yourself.*
> *Utilize this plan in establishing intermediate goals to help you achieve success.*
> *Utilize the pulling power of your goal gradient.*

Your *goal gradient* will give you the pulling power to accomplish your over-all goal—successfully.

Remember:

Know you have a goal.

Know what that goal is.

Get to that goal the most efficient way possible, by setting intermediate goals and thus using your goal gradient.

MEMORY METER

100%	
90%	
80%	
70%	
60%	
50%	Goal Setting
40%	Mental Hooks
30%	Mood Mastery
20%	Memory Motive
10%	Normal Usage

REWARD YOURSELF

Every day learns from that which preceded it.
Publilius Syrus: *Sententiae.*

Remember the story of the man who went on the wagon? He carefully passed every bar on his way home in the evening. But, after he
had passed by the last obstacle to his staying on the wagon, and was
safely on the last leg home, he turned back to the bar he had just
passed and went in to have a drink.

His reasoning was that he deserved a *reward* for having
accomplished what he had set out to do.

Sure, it is a humorous story—but it has the essence of one
of remembering's greatest secret aids: *reward.*

Reward is the least known of the memory aids. Yet its importance is so great that it can spell the difference between failure and
success.

REINFORCEMENT BY REWARD

Just as success is rewarding, so you must use the principle of
reward in creating and abetting your successes.

This is the principle of Reinforcement by Reward.

The rule you have to apply is simply this: *Remembering is
reinforced by rewarding.*

"What do you mean by 'reward yourself'?" the master of ceremonies of a popular television interview once asked me. "Can't that become an expensive proposition?"

I had to laugh at the impression this man had received from the word "reward."

In the first place, the reward you use is nothing more than a simple, everyday something that if it were not used as your reward would actually be a distraction in your process of remembering.

Second, your reward can only become "expensive" in the sense that you are gaining nothing by it and, in fact, losing something because of it—if you use it at the wrong time.

At this point, I want you to stop for a moment and try to remember just what happened while you were reading the previous chapter of this book.

I want you to answer these questions:

1. Did you read the chapter right through without any interruption that took your mind off the subject? _____
2. Did you stop reading for a few minutes to make yourself a cup of coffee? _____
3. Did you pause in your reading to make a phone call to someone you had intended to call during the day? _____
4. Did you turn on the television set or the radio to listen to your favorite program or to watch the ball game for a few minutes? _____
5. Did you set the book down while you looked into the candy box and selected a bonbon to eat? _____

Take your pencil and write your "yes" or "no" answer in the space beside each question, now!

WHAT WERE YOUR DISTRACTIONS? _____

You have written "yes" or "no" to the five questions. What were your answers? They are significant, because they indicate whether you are being distracted in your progress—and whether your distractions can be turned into favorable, reward-giving pleasures.

If you answered "yes" to any one or more of questions Nos. 2 to 5, you have suffered in the complete absorption of your reading, by interruption.

If you answered "no" to question No. 1, and "no" to all the other questions, write down right here the reason for which you voluntarily interrupted your reading.

_____

_____

_____

_____

If you answered "yes" to any of the questions Nos. 2 to 5, go back with your pencil and underline the question or questions so answered. This will make the cause of your distraction stand out sharply to your eye. This was the distracting influence in your work during the last chapter.

Can you prevent distractions? More important, can you use them to reward yourself?

The answer to these two questions is the key to giving you the power to remember successfully.

The answer is the key to helping you achieve greater success in everything you do.

The answer is the key to helping you retain your improved memory-efficiency.

The answer is the key to helping you create for yourself and utilize for your own benefit the power to remember successfully—a power that will never leave you, that will never fail you, that will heighten all the powers of your brain.

Distraction is a negative factor in remembering.

Why?

Simply because your train of thought is interrupted at the wrong time. Simply because your chain of remembering is broken by a weak link.

What can be done to turn this weak link into a postive factor of remembering?

PAYING THE REWARD

Make use of the very distraction—the cup of coffee, the telephone call, the bonbon—as you reward when you have completed what you set out to do.

In other words, don't stop for that piece of candy; don't turn on the radio or television set; don't give in to the negative factor . . . until you have finished your prescribed task.

While reading this book, if—as you should be doing—you are reading one chapter each day to improve your power to remember successfully, you must not interrupt yourself until the chapter is completely read. Then, and only then, may you drink the cup of coffee you thought you'd like to have; then may you make that phone call.

In this way the negative factor becomes the positive factor. The distracting influence is utilized by a complete reversal. Instead of detracting from your power to remember, it spurs you onward and rewards you for having increased that vital power.

Just how far can you go in making these rewards to yourself? There is a limit, obviously. The reward can be such that it will take you out of the actual learning situation. You will break the thread of your retention pattern and make useless everything that went before.

Don't take yourself away from the situation. Don't allow the reward to interrupt the benefit of the remembering you have done to gain that reward.

BEWARE OF DECREASED ATTENTION _____

One of the biggest factors in decreased efficiency of remembering is decreased attention. What causes this decreased attention? Competing motives are the culprits. They interfere with the task you have set out for yourself.

So it is that the thought of being hungry, or of having a letter to write or a phone call to make, competes with your desire to increase your memory-efficiency.

By bringing that competing factor into use in a positive fashion, you give yourself the reward you require to encourage your remembering. But you must be on your honor to yourself. You cannot take the reward for yourself unless you have first accomplished that which you have set out to accomplish.

When you feel that you have achieved perfection in what you were to do—when you have learned what you wanted to learn, recited it and know that it is established in your memory—then you may have the cup of coffee, or the piece of candy, or make the telephone calls, or whatever.

Remember, however, you must not let the reward take you too far away from the situation. That is, don't allow the reward to become a distraction again rather than a reward.

A reward such as going to the window to look out for a few minutes or to take a few breaths of fresh air can be sufficient to spur you on. It is especially good because it doesn't remove you from the situation.

I especially remember one student in a psychology class I taught who told me that she had taken my idea of rewarding oneself quite seriously. But, she told me, it didn't work too well for her.

"What was the reward you took for yourself and at what point in your studying did you take it?" I asked.

"After I read one chapter of a two-chapter section in history which I had to prepare for the next day, I went to a movie," was her sincere—and uncomprehending—reply.

Going to a movie, or any such activity that is going to take your mind completely away from what you are doing, is a distraction that will ruin the success of any effort on your part to increase your power of remembering.

DON'T DELAY YOUR REWARD

But, *you must not delay your reward.*

That is to say, you must not decide that your reward for having accomplished what you set out to do can be taken at a later time. If, for example, you are going to drink a cup of coffee after having read and absorbed this chapter, do it as soon as you *have* read and absorbed the chapter.

Delaying a reward is the surest way of decreasing—or nullifying—its effectiveness.

The best way of making your goal of value to you is by taking your reward as soon as possible after the accomplishment of that goal.

The reason you must not delay is that the psychological value of the reward tends to attach itself to whatever thing immediately preceded it.

You probably know what happens in the similar situation of punishment. Let us say a child has been naughty. One parent decides not to punish the child at that moment but says "Wait until Daddy (or Mommy) comes home!"

When the other parent comes home, it is his or her job to administer the punishment. What happens in the child's mind? Does the child associate the punishment with the naughtiness of several hours before? No, children tend to associate the punishment with the punishing parent. Its value as punishment is lost, because its point has been lost.

The same is true with reward. To get the value of its psychological effectiveness, reward yourself as soon as you have accomplished your goal. *But not before.*

The psychologist A. Jersild some years ago tried an experiment that showed that experiences with a pleasant memory—such as the reward that ties into what you are doing—are more easily retained than those with an unpleasant memory.

A group of fifty-one college students were asked to record in writing, as rapidly and comprehensively as possible, all the pleasant experiences they could remember having happened to them in the previous three weeks. They were allowed seven minutes to write this report.

After they finished the report and turned the papers in, the group were asked to write down all the unpleasant experiences they had had in the same period. This too took seven minutes and these papers were collected.

Nothing more was said of the task until twenty-one days later. At that time, the group were asked—without warning—to repeat the same work. This gave the experimenter two recalls—the original one and the one three weeks later. The results were as follows:

	Average number of:	
	Pleasant Experiences	*Unpleasant Experiences*
First recall	16.35	13.7
Recall 21 days later	7.0	3.86

Jersild noted that not only had a greater number of pleasant experiences been remembered at the initial writing, but the proportion of pleasant experiences retained for three weeks was greater than the unpleasant ones.

The experiment showed that 42.81 per cent of the pleasant experiences originally reported were remembered at second recall.

But for the unpleasant experiences, only 28.18 per cent of those originally reported were remembered later.

So reward has a psychological value in helping make your remembering experiences pleasant ones—and therefore rememberable ones.

But reward has its place. It must not interrupt your remembering process.

REWARD, REMINISCE, REMEMBER

The time you use in taking your reward has been found to be very valuable time. It is valuable to you, if you take your reward after you have reached your goal. It will be costly to you if you take your reward before you have reached the goal.

Despite what many people may think and say about such reward-interruptions, the time they utilize is not wasted. Science has proved that this time—the time you take out to have a cup of coffee or look out of the window—is a time in which you are learning.

"Isn't that rather unusual?" the sales manager of a large firm asked me.

"No," was my answer. "It is not unusual. It is the phenomenon called *reminiscence*."

I went on to explain what reminiscence is and how it works. And what I told this man—a martinet when it came to seeing that he worked every moment of the hours he spent in his office; and he demanded the same of his staff—shocked him. He was amazed at the results of experiments that showed the phenomenon of reminiscence.

Best of all, though, was that he became convinced that a properly timed break in any task is the secret for getting improved results out of the human brain.

JUST WHAT IS REMINISCENCE?

The curious phenomenon of reminiscence was first discovered in experiments that sought to determine how soon after learning something it is forgotten. Experiment showed that unless there had been review, under normal circumstances whatever was learned was rapidly forgotten.

But, upon closer examination, the experimenters found that for a short time after the person first acquired the learning, the memory was greater than it had been upon immediately acquiring the learning. The two tables that follow illustrate clearly this unusual phenomenon, of which you will take advantage to increase your power to remember successfully.

The experimenters asked themselves two questions:

1. Is it possible to remember more than you have learned?
2. Can the brain retain something more than it had acquired in the first place?

The suggestions were absurd. More detailed study was made, therefore, into the phenomenon.

The results were utterly amazing!

The British psychologist, P. B. Ballard, in an experiment involving 12-year-olds who were accustomed to learning poetry as a regular part of their school work, found that reminiscence increased their memory-efficiency for several days after they first learned a poem.

By establishing a "norm" for the amount the children were able to remember immediately after they first learned the poem and calling it 100, this is what Dr. Ballard found:

Immediately after learning 100
After one day the average was 111
After two days the average was 117
After three days the average was 113
After four days the average was 112
After five days the average was 111
After six days the average was 99
After seven days the average was 94

You see that for the five days immediately after the children learned the poetry, the reminiscence effect increased their memory power to a point beyond the original memory.

MORE PROOF OF REMINISCENCE POWER

Another psychological experimenter, F. Nicolai, used a group of objects in a box. He lifted the lid of the box for about fifteen seconds to allow his subjects to look into it. Immediately upon closing the lid, he then asked the subjects to recall what they had seen in the box. He also repeated the question at various intervals after the initial exposure. His average for a group of people who were shown a box containing ten objects showed the reminiscence effect.

The Nicolai experiment results averaged as follows:

Time Elapsed After Seeing Objects	Number of Objects Remembered
Immediately	5.4
Half-hour	5.1
One hour	6.3
Five hours	7.0
Twenty-four hours	7.8
Four days	7.6
Four weeks	7.4

Innumerable other experiments show the existence of reminiscence.

By using the first rule you have learned in this chapter— *Remembering is reinforced by rewarding*—you will permit yourself and your wonderful brain machine time for reminiscence to take place. Then, having allowed the phenomenon of reminiscence to work for you, you can continue in your plan to increase your power of remembering whatever it is you are trying to remember.

Remember:

Remembering is reinforced by rewarding.

Rewarding allows time for reminiscence to take place.

Reminiscence is a plus in the power to remember.

MEMORY METER

100%	
90%	
80%	
70%	
60%	Reward Giving
50%	Goal Setting
40%	Mental Hooks
30%	Mood Mastery
20%	Memory Motive
10%	Normal Usage

8

THE SPACING SPEEDUP

Memory is like a purse—if it be over-full that it cannot shut, all will drop out of it.
Thomas Fuller: *Holy and Profane States.*

The next step in increasing your memory-efficiency successfully combines the phenomenon of reminiscence with another important key in remembering.

This key is called "spacing."

This is the key that will make your memory work for you more simply, more efficiently, and with greater speed.

You have already discovered the remembering powers of reminiscence. Now you are going to see how by using the theory of spacing—or *spaced learning*—you can increase and encourage your reminiscence to the point of bringing you a full step nearer perfection of memory-efficiency—full usage of your power to remember successfully.

You now know about the phenomenon of reminiscence. You realize that for some time after you first try to remember something, your brain will produce for your conscious memory more of what you learned than it did immediately after you first learned it.

REMINISCENCE AND SPACED LEARNING

Can reminiscence be used to even greater advantage?

Yes—and with fabulous results!

99

The theory of spaced learning fits right into the phenomenon of reminiscence like a key does into its lock.

Let us assume, for example, that you are in a telephone booth. You are talking to a business acquaintance who tells you of someone who can give you a big order if you call right away. You are happy at this contact. It isn't every day you walk unexpectedly into a large order without having had to work for it.

You reach into your pocket and discover that there is no ink in your pen. You cannot write the telephone number down—and yet you must remember it.

You repeat the number that your friend has given you. But will you remember it through the balance of the conversation? Will it remain with you long enough for you to make the phone call to this person? What if the line is busy? Will you remember it so that you can call again in a few minutes?

It seems like a small thing—only a telephone number. Not much to remember—but how many times have you had the unfortunate experience of forgetting a telephone number you had just been told?

Your usual procedure in remembering a telephone number is to repeat it a few times to yourself as soon as you have heard it. Then, off you go with whatever you were doing. But when the time comes to dial the number—*you can't recall it.*

The way to overcome this problem is by spaced learning.

THE FIRST RULE OF SPACING

The rule of space learning is: *A moment's rest is worth two moments' cramming.*

In other words, after you have once repeated the telephone number—or whatever it is you wish to remember—pause for a short time and then repeat it the second time. Then pause again before repeating it a third time.

Each pause allows the number to sink deeper into your memory and increases your power to remember it. Each pause encourages your brain to utilize the phenomenon of reminiscence and thus produce even greater memory-efficiency.

What happens if, for instance, you have to remember a list of points for a speech you have to make? How do you make your spaced learning and your reminiscence work to your advantage?

Let us take an example to see what results you get.

Below is a list of words that are the key words in a speech. They are related one to the other so that remembering them should not be a difficult thing to do.

Read the list of words and reread over and over until you can recall all of them without looking at the list. This is the method called "massed learning."

Time yourself and write down in the space provided at the end of the list how long it took you to remember the entire list.

1. Current political scene
2. Domestic affairs
3. International relationships
4. Presidential powers
5. Suggested constitutional reforms

*Time required to remember completely:*_____

TEST THE VALUE OF SPACING _____

Now, having completed this test on the value of "massed learning," test the value of spaced learning. Here, again, is a list of words that will serve as the remembering-key to a speech you are going to make.

This time read the list once and then look away from it for about ten seconds. Read the list a second time and try to recall it. If you have not remembered it accurately, look away for ten seconds again and then read it for a third time. Continue the process until you can recall the list without error. Now write down the time it took.

1. Uses of atomic energy
2. Role in national defense
3. Destructive potential
4. Reactor dangers
5. Future in nuclear world ?

*Time required to remember completely:*_____
Which list took less time?

The first list acquired by "massed learning" was probably less readily remembered than the second list on which you used spaced learning—even though there were ten-second intervals between reading. All experiments have shown that spaced learning is more advantageous than massed learning.

The spacing between readings, allowing what is to be remembered some time to sink in—aided by the phenomenon of reminiscence—is going to give you better results in every instance and help you to make another step up the ladder to successful memory-efficiency.

What happens when you use the method of "massed learning" when you are trying to remember a telephone number? You are using what psychologists call a "primary memory image," and nothing more. You are not really learning at all.

MEMORY ECHO IS AN ILLUSION _____

In all of our senses there is what is known as a "memory echo." That is to say, the sense organ involved continues to respond after the stimulus has stopped.

A common example of how this "memory echo" works can be recalled if you think of the last time you looked at an electric light bulb as you turned off the power. The eye continues to see the light for a fraction of a second after the current no longer is illuminating the filament in the bulb.

Another example you have undoubtedly experienced is having someone hit you on the ear. Even though the sound of the contact is momentary, you seem to continue hearing sound for a short time after the blow.

You have often experienced this memory echo with a person who is speaking and to whom you are paying little attention. If that person stops speaking, you still continue to hear for a second or more. It is this memory echo that may have come to your rescue when you were a student at school.

If you had not been paying attention to what the teacher was saying and were suddenly asked a question, chances are that your memory echo served you well in allowing you to recall what the question was so that you could answer it.

The echo, the responding of the sense organ, however, would not work if the teacher had paused after making the last statement and before asking you the question. Inasmuch as it is not memory but an echo, the pause would provide no echo for your ear to respond to.

What happens, then, if you try to remember a telephone number by the massed-learning method? You are just hearing—or recalling—because of the echo and not because of your memory-efficiency.

In the case of the telephone number, all that massed learning will do is give you a sure echo by the time you get to the telephone to dial. But if you get a busy signal and have to dial the number later, chances are that you will have forgotten it.

THE ADVANTAGE OF SPACING _____

When is spaced learning of advantage to you? The spaced-learning method is useful when you have to remember some such thing as a list, a number, names—anything that you would ordinarily attempt to remember by cram-memory or massed learning. It allows time for matter that might interfere to dissipate from your memory.

Let us say you are at a convention and you meet three dozen persons. You know that eighteen of these people will be of help to you and you want to remember their names.

At the time that you are introduced to a person you know you are going to want to recall later, repeat the name in the introduction and then, within the first few minutes that follow, repeat the name to yourself silently every thirty seconds or so.

You will find that you have had little trouble in remembering all the names of all the persons you want to remember.

However, after you have returned home from your gathering, run over the names of those persons you want to remember and note them down. The next day, run over the list again. You will find that in addition to the advantages of the spaced-learning method, you will also reap the profits of your power of reminiscence.

AVOID INTERFERENCE _____

At the very start in spacing, be sure that you don't encounter the interference of having other important things compete for your remembering power. After you have repeated the names—or whatever it is you need to remember—a second or third time, there is less chance of interference spoiling your remembering.

In fact, the chances are that whatever the interference was it will dissipate within the next day, and whatever you had to remember will remain more vivid.

As you saw in Chapter 7 on rewarding yourself, your power of reminiscence increases your memory-efficiency on the second day. Let us say, then, that you are studying Spanish as preparation for a business trip to Mexico and you have set for yourself a program of learning twenty-five words a day over a period of time.

The first time you start working on a twenty-five-word list you will find that you may recall twenty immediately. By the process of reminiscence you will find that perhaps twenty-two of them are fresh in your mind the day after. Starting at that point—with spaced learning as your method of approach—you are two words ahead of yourself as you review the first list for the first time.

With that in mind you can see how easily you are going to reach each day's quota to perfection within a few days of review of each specific list.

Utilize your remembering time to its best advantage, too, by keeping your spaced learning periods of each day as close together as possible. If you don't, you will waste a great deal of time in preliminaries.

THE WARM-UP

Wasting time in this fashion will make you a *warm-up waster.*

Each time you go back to your remembering session there takes place a *warm-up.* Because of this you must not be fooled into allowing yourself too great a period of rest, relaxation, or reward between periods of remembering. You must utilize your spaced learning time to its fullest.

If you have to warm up for too long you are going to be spending minutes foolishly.

You know how you have to get into the swing of whatever you were doing, once you have stopped and before you can set off at full pace again.

You know how baseball pitchers throw three or four pitches before starting each inning. Despite the fact that they have worked out carefully before the game and are in the best physical shape for that contest, nonetheless they loosen their throwing muscles before facing a new batch of opponents in each inning.

The pitcher's warm-up is no different from the one you

undergo each time you go back to your remembering in utilizing spaced learning. If the "inning" in your remembering has been short, the period of warm-up is shorter. If you are only "pitching" once a day, you have to go through the entire pre-game warm-up each day.

DON'T BE A WARM-UP WASTER _____

A lawyer I know once disputed this argument with me. He felt that a certain few preliminary steps should be taken before a person gets down to working at anything. Only a day later I had occasion to be at his office and pointed out to him that it was more than ten minutes after I sat down at his desk before he was ready to discuss what I had come to talk to him about.

There were pencils to be sharpened. A file to be found. A pair of books to be sent for. A telephone call to be made.

When he became aware of this warm-up waste my lawyer friend admitted that there might be something in my theory.

If you are getting prepared for a day's program of remembering, get everything that you need together before you start. That will make it unnecessary for you to jump up to get a blotter, a glass of water, a piece of paper, or what-have-you.

Put everything you are going to need in a handy spot near you. This will prevent a lengthy warm-up and help you get into the swing of your remembering with a minimum of interference and delay.

A good idea is to prepare at the start of any remembering project a list of all the things you need. Keep that list on your desk and refer to it every day before you start to work.

Head it *"My Warm-Up List."* Write down in order of their use whatever you are going to use.

For instance, if you are going to prepare yourself for a new sales trip with the seasonal line your firm has put out, your list might read this way:

MY WARM-UP LIST

Memo pad
New Catalog

Old Catalog
Pencils (black, red, and blue)
Order book
Buyers' list
Railroad timetable
Hotel list

In that way, you can set about remembering your new sales promotion program and plan your trip without having to get up from your desk or chair; you can avoid the interference that would hinder your remembering.

SPACED VS. MASSED LEARNING _____

Why is spaced learning preferable to massed learning?

Aside from the advantages already listed, there is one more major factor that has to be taken into consideration. That is the false security that massed learning gives.

Let us go back to that telephone number you were trying to remember a few pages back. Suppose you just repeated it over and over three or four times and then walked off.

You would be sure that you would never forget that number because you had just said it three or four times without a hitch. You didn't forget a single digit of it, you didn't get mixed up, you didn't even forget whose number it is, did you?

But you did do one thing. You led yourself into a bit of false security.

You think you know the number because of the memory image. You didn't have a moment to lose that image. The memory echo was repeating the number as you last said it, right back into your mind's ear.

But a half hour later, the number is gone. The remembering effort has been a total loss—and it can be a loss in many more ways than in just not recalling a phone number.

Of course, as we indicated before, spaced learning is an advantage in learning complicated material as well.

If you are trying to learn something of any length, you are best off adopting the method of spaced learning. In other words, rest a few moments between each repetition. However, if the spacing is too wide, the rest intervals will act as interference rather than as aids to memory.

SHOULD YOU CRAM?

There are two schools of thought when it comes to the system of cramming to help you remember.

> *1. There are those who say that cramming is the best type of remembering.*
> *2. There are those who say that cramming is the worst type of remembering.*

In a sense, both schools of thought are right. It all depends on what you are trying to remember and why.

What are the advantages of cramming?

If you want to remember something just for a short time, then the cram method of learning will probably be just the thing you want.

In the cram method, your learning is jammed into a short space of time. Shortly after it has been learned, you can remember it. Shortly after you have remembered it for whatever specific purpose you had, you will forget it.

Generally, if you are trying to improve your memory-efficiency, if you are trying to increase your power to remember successfully, and to make the fullest use of that power, the cram method is the wrong approach to remembering.

Its disadvantages are too great. Your power to remember becomes weakened by the fact that everything you stuffed into yourself to remember soon disappears from your memory.

If, however, you do require to remember something just for a short time—to answer questions on an examination, to supply information for an application, to present a summary of some research to a club meeting—you can utilize the effects of sleep memory to make cramming most effective.

REMEMBERING WHILE YOU SLEEP

Psychological experiments have shown that when you awaken after sleep—since you obviously have had less interference with your remembering process—you can recall greater amounts than you could if instead of sleeping you had been awake the same number of hours.

The Psychologist, E. B. van Ormer, in a series of experiments, discovered that on the average a person's remembering held almost steady after a seven-hour sleep period. But it decreased to almost half in the same number of waking hours, the experiment showed.

The same experiment was tried with cockroaches—probably one of the few times that these insects have ever been put to any gainful use—and the results were almost identical.

The conclusion that forgetting is slow during sleeptime—or rapid during daytime activity—can be accepted with only a few reservations. It is true that material that has been barely learned follows this pattern most closely—cramming is certainly "barely" learning.

If you must cram, review right before going to sleep, and, if possible, again right before you use the crammed material. In this way you have the best chance to remember it.

By properly spacing your remembering process and by keying the entire process to your period of sleep, you can reach the next rung on the ladder to the power of remembering.

Remember:

Spacing helps reminiscence.

Spacing and reminiscence increase memory-efficiency.

Don't be a warm-up waster.

Don't cram, unless you don't want to retain permanently.

MEMORY METER

100%	
90%	
80%	
70%	Spacing Speedup
60%	Reward Giving
50%	Goal Setting
40%	Mental Hooks
30%	Mood Mastery
20%	Memory Motive
10%	Normal Usage

The Eighth Day

A BIRD'S-EYE VIEW

The one who weaves his experiences into systematic relations with each other will be the one with the best memory.
William James: *Psychology.*

When you were a child, how did you memorize poetry?

Did you, as so many of us were inclined to do, learn a stanza at a time? Or did you try to learn the entire poem without breaking it up into sections?

A common way to teach children poetry is the first method I mentioned. But experiments have shown that this is usually not the best method for remembering.

One remembers most easily—if you will recall what we discussed earlier—when the meaning is most vivid. To break up meaningful material into parts is to lose the cohesiveness that would make the remembering all the easier.

However, not all the meaning and ability to remember is lost by division.

A COMBINATION OF WHOLE AND PART

In order to reach the next step on the ladder to success on the Memory Meter, you must learn to use a combination of both methods of learning—the whole and the part.

If what you have to remember is not too long, it is best that you try to remember it as a whole. It has more meaning that way—it is more vivid and therefore is more rememberable.

If what you have to remember is too long to tackle by the whole method, it should be understood as a "whole" first. In that way the initial meaningfulness is there. Then it should be broken into as few parts as possible.

So that you can fully understand the necessity for this, let us recall your experiences in school days. You remember, as you recalled a moment ago, how you learned poetry in school.

You had a long poem to memorize and so after school one day you learned the first stanza. Then you went out to play. The second day you learned the second stanza; and so on. On the day you learned the last stanza you thought, most likely, that you had memorized the entire poem.

You had reason to believe this. Hadn't you been able to repeat a new stanza at the end of each day? Weren't you able to recite it letter-perfect, and now wouldn't you be able to recite the entire poem stanza by stanza?

So, came the day when you had to do your recitation and what happened? You sailed off into the first stanza like a four-masted schooner before a strong wind—to the end of the first stanza. Came the second stanza and the wind wasn't there. The sails sagged and the ship slid to a stop.

Your memory balked. The second stanza—which you could recite without a mishap on the second day of your learning chore—just wasn't there.

What happened? How can we explain this blank?

Psychologists describe it as a lack of association. In other words, the meaningfulness of the whole poem wasn't there. You found association between the lines of each stanza. But you did nothing to link each stanza with the next.

You learned the first, and left it at that. The next day, you started from scratch at the second. What was there to link the last line of the first stanza,

"And things are not what they seem,"

with the first line of the second stanza,

"Life is real! Life is earnest!"

Certainly, if by any chance you had today to sit down and learn Alfred Lord Tennyson's "Break, break, break," you wouldn't try to do it line by line or bit by bit. By way of clearing the ground and preparing the way to remembering the poem, you would read it through carefully first.

This would give you a unified impression of the poem—it would present the entire work in its over-all vividness. You would search for, and find, the continuous thread of meaning that runs through it and holds it together.

After that, the various details would be brought into place, polished, and perfected.

GET THE BIRD'S-EYE VIEW

The same approach holds true no matter what it is you are going to remember.

You must get the over-all picture in your mind.

This is the *Bird's-Eye View.*

If the over-all picture is too long, then, to swallow in a single gulp of memory, divide it into practical parts. But make sure that each of the parts has some cohesiveness and definite association with the parts preceding and following it.

The ability to give cohesiveness to each segment of what you are remembering—and to create an association with the other segments—is well illustrated in a story told about the late general and statesman, George C. Marshall.

Marshall, at a press conference during World War II, met with some sixty correspondents. He decided that it would be easiest if they were to ask all their questions first; he would then answer each in turn without interruption.

The correspondents started their questioning—each asking one question. At the end of the query period, Marshall started to talk and continued for forty minutes without a break. He answered, in order, each man's question—his *Bird's-Eye View* of the conference making one cohesive picture of the questions he had been asked.

To make the interview that much more astounding, Marshall even had tied-in the face of each correspondent with the question, and directed the proper answer to each man by looking at him.

General Marshall at a later date astounded a Congressional committee by testifying before it without a single note. He spoke quite informally, yet answered every question with an obvious memory of all the facts he had to draw upon.

Again it was his *Bird's-Eye View* of the subject he was talking on that enabled him to tie-in for his memory's use all the facts and present them in a clear manner.

The tieing-in process is one that is used, too, in remembering large groups of people. This is the secret of the so-called memory experts who perform their parlor tricks of memory as a life's work. You can develop this ability by using the trick of "making it meaningful" and the system of *Bird's-Eye Viewing* to tie-in people, giving them cohesiveness and meaning in your memory.

So, you see, even when it comes to remembering people, it is best to use the method of whole and part.

BE PREPARED FOR YOUR TASK _____

You have often heard the now-no-longer-funny stories of plumbers who forget their tools. This is the sort of wastefulness that learning in parts brings. It is the wastefulness of having to stop from time to time to hunt up the needed "tools" instead of having the entire "tool chest" at hand.

Have you ever watched two students at work preparing a lesson in which one is completely set to study and the other is totally unprepared?

The second starts the assignment and then decides to take notes. The student doesn't have a notebook or pen, and so must stop to get them. A few minutes later the student discovers the pen has run out of ink. Where is another one? Later the same student realizes it is uncomfortable to study in hiking boots. It is time to take a break to change his shoes.

When at last the assignment has been completely read, this student complains that he or she hasn't the slightest idea what it was all about. Do you wonder? The frequent breaks in thought from all the interruptions so broke up continuity, that the reading was about as meaningful as a list of nonsense syllables.

Too many people do not know how to set about learning the things that they desire to remember. They may see the meaning. They may concentrate. They may even have great interest. Yet they do not know the best way to use their power to remember successfully.

HOW TO SAVE TIME

Repeated tests show that a twenty-per-cent saving in the time that is needed to remember completely can be achieved by "whole" learning in contrast to "part" learning.

The most famous is that of a young man who was given two poetry passages, each two hundred forty lines long. He studied one by the whole method and the other by the part method.

The experiment required him to study for thirty-five minutes a day until the lines were learned. The actual results were:

Method of Study	Days Required	Total Minutes Required
30 lines a day; then whole reviewed until it could be recited	12	431
3 readings of whole a day until it could be recited	10	348

The *Bird's-Eye View* method gave an economy of eighty-three minutes over the part method.

But other experiments, depending upon the length of the work to be remembered, showed that the part method was more economical.

What, then, is the best thing to do?

Instead of slavishly following a mechanical rule, adapt the rules to your own circumstances.

If what you have to remember is short, or comparatively short, try to remember it as a whole.

If what you have to remember is long, get the *Bird's-Eye View* and then remember it in sections that are as large as possible, each time tying-in section with section.

In either method you must use a principle of remembering that plays a great part in the ease of learning. What you learn first is easiest remembered; what you learn last is next easiest recalled; and what you learned in the middle is the most difficult to recall.

Psychologists call this the rule of Primacy and Recency. I prefer to have you remember it as the *BEM* rule—the *Beginning,* the *End,* and the *Middle.*

What can you gain by knowing this rule of ease of learning? Simply this: by realizing that what you learn in the middle is least likely to stay with you, you can avoid the pitfall of forgetting it. You can put a greater amount of time into learning the middle portion.

In other words, watch the middle—the ends will take care of themselves.

THE WHOLE, THE PART, AND THIS BOOK _____

This book was written in such a manner that you would benefit by the combination of "whole" and "part."

Inasmuch as it is best to get a vivid over-all picture of what you are learning and remembering, and then to divide the work up into natural sections for easier retention, this book was written with a *Bird's-Eye View* chapter at the beginning.

What did that chapter do? Why is it different?

In the first place, the *Bird's-Eye View* chapter gave you an over-all summary of what you were going to gain by reading this book. It presented for you a vivid impression of how you were going to increase your power to remember successfully.

In that way it was not necessary for you to waste time first reading through the entire volume to understand it and then going back to benefit by each chapter, one by one.

The uniqueness in this presentation is that in most other books a summary is given at the end. After you have worked your way through without the benefit of an over-all picture, the author comes along with a summation that would have best been written at the front of the book.

In this book, you have been shown how the "whole" and "part" methods fit together for your greatest advantage. The whole is presented as a summary at the start of the book. The parts are each chapter, each tied in carefully to the last, each a complete whole in itself to make your power to remember an easier and more accomplishable thing.

Remember:

Get a vivid, *Bird's-Eye View* impression of the whole.

Make a logical division into learnable parts.

See that each part is a self-contained whole.

Get your parts to hang together by association.

With these four rules of whole and part learning, you are only two steps away from accomplishing the final goal—successful use of your power to remember.

MEMORY METER

100%	
90%	
80%	Bird's-Eye View
70%	Spacing Speedup
60%	Reward Giving
50%	Goal Setting
40%	Mental Hooks
30%	Mood Mastery
20%	Memory Motive
10%	Normal Usage

10

The Ninth Day

THE KEY
TO PERMANENT
MEMORY

*The jar will long retain the fragrance with which
it was steeped when new.*
Horace: *Epistles.*

One of the fundamental ways of learning that you used in your
school days is the key to successfully using the power of remembering in a more permanent fashion.

It is *recitation.*

Recitation is repeating to yourself, or to someone else, out
loud that which you are trying to remember. And it must be done
with the original material out of sight. Otherwise, you are likely to
try to cue yourself by peeking.

Attempting to recite out loud while you are in the process
of trying to remember is one of the greatest aids in achieving a permanence to the remembering.

Do not just read and reread what you are trying to remember. Recall, by recitation, as much as possible each time you go
through it.

116

THE THREE VALUES OF RECITATION _____

The recitation key has three main values:

1. It will assure you of saving time in several ways.
2. It will show you which sections you are having trouble in remembering.
3. It will assure greater permanence to the remembering.

Saving time sounds odd to you, perhaps. But recitation is a time-saver. It saves time in two important ways:

1. You will have concrete proof that you have entirely and successfully remembered what you set out to remember when you can recite it fully.
2. You will economize in the amount of time it takes to accomplish the successful memorizing.

Again you may feel puzzled. How can there be an economy of time by recitation? This has been thoroughly tested by experiment. The results of the experiments have shown that recitation methods are by far the faster when it comes to remembering.

The results of one experiment, done some years ago, can be shown in the chart reproduced on the next page.

The time devoted to study in each case in the experiment was nine minutes. This time was divided between reading and recitation in the proportions as listed in the first column of the chart.

The subjects in each case had a sheet of paper before them containing the lesson to be studied; they simply read until they were told to recite. When they started to recite, they consulted the paper as often as was necessary and continued this way until the end of the study period.

As you can see the nonsense-syllable remembering increased from thirty-five per cent to seventy-four per cent upon immediate testing, after four-fifths of the time was spent in recitation. After four hours the increase was from fifteen to forty-eight per cent.

In the case of the short biographies, the maximum recitation-time value seemed to be achieved when three-fifths of the

MATERIAL STUDIED

	16 nonsense syllables		5 short biographies (about 170 words total)	
Distribution of Learning Time	% Immedi- ately	% After 4 hours	% Immedi- ately	% After 4 hours
All time devoted to reading	35	15	35	16
1/5 time devoted to recitation	50	26	37	19
2/5 time devoted to recitation	54	28	41	25
3/5 time devoted to recitation	57	37	42	26
4/5 time devoted to recitation	74	48	42	26

time was spent in that fashion. The increase from thiry-five to forty-two per cent is noted for the immediate recall with the increase going from sixteen to twenty-six per cent after four hours.

RECITATION PROVES ITS WORTH

Two important facts stand out from this experimental study. First, recitation proved to be an advantage in all cases. Second, the advantage was present not only for immediate remembering—but also for remembering over a period of time.

The proof is positive: *Recitation favors permanent memory.*

Why is there an advantage to recitation?

Primarily because it is more stimulating than the continued rereading of the same lesson.

The simple rereading of whatever it is you have to commit to memory can easily degenerate into a meaningless reading of words. This contributes very little toward realizing and learning the sense of what you are trying to remember.

Each time you recite, however, you discover just how much you already know and just what demands close attention. It makes you more observant.

So the rule of observation comes into play again.

Remember: *To use the power of remembering, you have to be observant.*

If attempted too soon, of course, recitation can be a waste of your time. The material has to be explored carefully first—just as you do in getting a *Bird's-Eye View.*

Remember: *To use the power of remembering, you must understand the "whole" first.*

So explore and find out what your material contains, then reread, and then recite.

Recitation will give you a quick clue as to how much you *really* remember in contrast to what you may *believe* you remember. If, let us say, you are trying to remember material for a Civil Service examination, it is best to know before it is too late—that is, before writing the exam—that your knowledge of the subject could bear improving.

There is also a quicker emotional response in the recitation method. If you succeed in recalling as much as you hoped, there is immediate satisfaction.

Remember: *Reward encourages remembering.*

TRY READING ALOUD

There is another trick that will prove of great benefit to you in accomplishing your next step up to a successful memory.

Try reading aloud the material you are going to remember.

What does this do? Why does it help?

By reading aloud you get an entirely different picture of what you are learning. You get a sound picture.

When you read silently, the picture is a mental one. The words bear shape on the paper. The sentences have form on the paper. The meaning is one to the eye and the brain.

When you read aloud, the picture becomes a vivid one. The words bear shape in the imagination. The sentences take form in sound. The meaning is one for the ear, the eye, and the brain.

Most important is hearing your own voice say the words that you will be saying at some later date when you are going to use the knowledge you are now remembering.

The words take on new meaning when your own voice carries them. They have meaning for *you,* from *you.*

Reading aloud after a first survey reading, and then reciting, brings you a step closer to the final goal of total recall at a later date.

It is later that you want to be able to recall without any help whatsoever. In reciting you recall as much as possible without help. In reading aloud you get used to hearing the sound of your own voice saying the words you will want to say later.

It is but a short step from reading aloud, and reciting, to recalling without help or trickery of any sort.

If you are in a position where you cannot read it aloud, get pencil and paper and write it down. This is the next best thing to do.

Of course, all three methods put together are the prize package of recitation.

If at all possible follow this procedure:

1. *Read it aloud.*
2. *Recite it aloud.*
3. *Write it down.*

The effect will surprise you, for it brings rapid and successful memory.

WHAT ABOUT "OVERLEARNING"?

Continued recitation makes for a condition that the psychologists call "overlearning." In many ways it is a good thing.

Continued practice makes for the same effect.

You have seen that a list of nonsense syllables, even when learned to the point where they can be repeated correctly, will be forgotten if they are not needed again.

Yet there is no list of syllables more nonsensical than the twenty-six that make up the English alphabet. There is no logical connection between the letters. The syllables as such have little or no meaning. Even if you want to think of those letters of the alphabet that can be given meaning—such as "a," "b" (bee), "c" (sea), "i," "j" (jay), "l" (ell), "o," "p" (pea), "q" (cue), "r" (are), "t" (tea), "u" (you), and "y" (why)—there still is no logical connection between the words.

Yet you can go for days, weeks, or months, without using the alphabet as such, or even using a dictionary. Nevertheless you never forget it. It has become so much a part of us that the story told of the librarian and her herb garden might well be true.

The story goes that a librarian lived in an apartment, but very much wanted to have a garden. She had a windowbox built so that she could at least grow a few herbs she particularly liked to use for cooking.

In the spring she planted seeds in the windowbox. A friend, surprised at how small the "garden" was, asked the librarian how she would know which herb was which in such a tiny space. The reply she received was:

"I planted them alphabetically."

When the need arises, any one of us can recite the alphabet without a hitch. In fact, the recitation comes so readily and smoothly, one might think that it had been part of a daily catechism all one's life.

It is the amount of practice of the original learning that has made the difference. Anything that is just barely learned and never used again will soon be forgotten, particularly if it has no logical connections or personal associations to make it stick in the mind.

But a little recitation aids retention and makes the power of remembering so much easier. And material that is "over-learned"—that is to say, repeated or reviewed many times past the point where you can repeat it correctly *once*—is retained so well that an ordinary lifetime is not long enough for it to be completely forgotten.

PROOF OF "OVERLEARNING" RETENTION

An experiment by psychologist W. C. F. Krueger some years ago showed that "overlearning" did actually increase retention. Krueger used twenty persons. He had them learn lists of twelve one-syllable nouns, such as barn, lamp, tree, chair, and so on.

Each list of nouns was shown in a series with each word visible for two seconds. The list was considered just learned when each person could go through it once without error. This was considered hundred-per-cent learning for each person. Then to determine the effects of "overlearning" Krueger decided that if it took ten times through the list to learn it one hundred per cent, fifteen times through a similar list would give one-hundred-fifty-per-cent learning—"overlearning" of fifty per cent.

The retention test was given at various intervals after the learning was finished. These intervals were one, two, four, seven, fourteen and twenty-eight days. The results of the retention tests are shown in the table on the next page.

The results show that fifty-per-cent "overlearning" was in every sense worth while, since it always gave at least fifty-per-cent better retention, and in most cases produced an increase exceeding that figure.

"Overlearning" plays a part in so many of our everyday activities. Skilled swimmers are said never to forget the art although they may go for years without swimming a stroke. Typists of many years' practice need only an hour or so to regain their former speed and skill at the typewriter. All such "overlearned" subjects are never really forgotten.

Length of Interval—Days	Degree of Learning—%	Average Number Words Recalled	Average % Words Recalled
1	100	3.10	25.83
	150	4.60	38.33
2	100	1.80	15.00
	150	3.60	30.00
4	100	0.50	4.17
	150	2.05	17.08
7	100	0.20	1.67
	150	1.30	10.83
14	100	0.15	1.25
	150	0.65	5.42
28	100	0.00	0.00
	150	0.25	2.08

DON'T BE FOOLED BY IMMEDIATE RECALL

You may often blame your memory—in reality, your power of retention—for the fact that you have forgotten something. The truth of the matter is that you have failed to learn it thoroughly in the first place. Or rather, you have failed to "overlearn" it.

If ten repetitions of a habit or a fact are necessary to learn it well enough for immediate recall, twenty repetitions may be necessary to fix it in your memory so that it can be recalled a month later. For permanent retention, perhaps thirty repetitions may be required.

Ability to recall immediately is no criterion of adequate learning.

The way to remember is to review. The time to review is early. The earlier the better, since the time immediately after you have first learned something is the time when it can be most easily forgotten—or most easily retained, if reviewed.

The best way to review is to make use of the practice of recitation. The best way to remember for life is to "overlearn."

The best kind of reviewing is that which comes from putting what you are trying to remember to some actual use. That gives your remembering power a more vivid and personal meaning to grasp.

You can recite something until you are able to remember it without having to refer to the original source. Or you can carry on and make absolutely certain of it.

You can continue beyond what appears to be immediately necessary. Such continuation does not occupy much additional time. Most of the time is spent in the earlier stages.

But "overlearning" is worth while. It helps the development of your power to remember.

Remember:

To use the power of remembering, you have to be observant.

To use the power of remembering, you have to understand the whole first.

Reward encourages remembering.

Recitation favors permanent memory.

"Overlearning" helps the development of your power to remember.

MEMORY METER

100%	
90%	Recitation
80%	Bird's-Eye View
70%	Spacing Speedup
60%	Reward Giving
50%	Goal Setting
40%	Mental Hooks
30%	Mood Mastery
20%	Memory Motive
10%	Normal Usage

The Tenth Day **11**

THE VALUE OF FORGETTING

Teach me the art of forgetting.
Cicero: *De Finibus.*

Your power to use your memory-efficiency successfully is given its biggest boost by one of the strangest faculties of the human mind—the ability to forget.

"Oh, but I forget very easily!" a charming woman cornered me with one day at a party after I had made the above statement. "Why is it then, that I can't remember very well? That seems to follow by your argument!"

What this scatterbrained woman failed to see was that she was forgetting the things she should have been remembering. That won't do anything for you at all—except keep you memory-inefficient.

The power to remember, the power to make a successful, dependable memory for yourself, rests last—and far from least—upon forgetting.

Contradictory as this may seem on the surface, it is so. It has been proven, it is being proven, it will be proven.

The last rule in increasing your power to remember to its full one hundred per cent is:

Don't clutter your mind with unimportant things—forget them!

One of the main reasons you have difficulty in remembering the specific things you wish to remember is the interference of other things that are presenting themselves to your memory. It is these extraneous things, this clutter, that you have to forget.

THE BEST WAY TO FORGET _____

What is the best way to forget?

By reversing the process of recitation and repetition you have the simplest and surest way of getting rid of the clutter of facts that will hinder your power of remembering successfully.

Tests have shown that the "curve of forgetting" is such that without the process of repetition you are likely to forget the greater proportion of material learned within one day.

This, then, is the secret to forgetting.

If the material you have heard or read is unimportant, if it has no value to you whatsoever, *do not repeat it or reread it.* By failing to give it a second chance in your memory, it will have lost out in the remembering process.

Valueless information, trivia, pointless facts—all can be hindrances to the value of your memory. All this worthless clutter can misemploy the power of your memory, creating interference with the retention of those things that you want to remember.

CAN YOU FORGET COMPLETELY? _____

There has been much controversy in the field of psychology as to whether the brain retains everything for all time.

Some psychologists, following the teachings of Sigmund Freud, feel that everything you learn, hear, read is always retained. They say that you forget nothing, only repress those things that you do not want to remember. To them, then, forgetting is repression.

Experiments on hypnosis seem to bear these theories out at times—but the experiments are often sketchy in their content, falling far short of thorough scientific proof. Hypnotists have often made a patient remember occurrences from childhood—but so often these occurrences are vivid spots in the child's life: a birthday party, a vacation trip, a shocking experience.

Recent books written on the powers of the brain tell the reader that the Unconscious—sometimes called the Subconscious or the Supraconscious—absorbs everything around us and retains it. With no more evidence than we have now, this statement seems extravagant.

It is highly probable that quite a lot is forgotten.

One of the chief causes of forgetting is interference—the very thing that helps hinder remembering.

A good example of the interference that causes forgetting is the one about remembering the name of a childhood friend. Let us say you had a schoolmate whose name was Norton. For years the name Norton signified that boy and no one else. But as time passed and he dropped out of your life and other "Nortons" came into your experience, the name almost (though not quite) lost its original meaning to you.

Interference in daily life is a common occurrence. Your everyday activities are alike in many ways. Certain experiences interfere with others that are similar, and the process of forgetting takes place.

DO YOU FORGET IN YOUR SLEEP?

Interference with memory is at a low level during sleep. This has been proved in many tests. Forgetting is less rapid during sleep than during waking hours. This was pointed out to you earlier in Chapter 4, "MASTERING YOUR MOODS," where it was shown that review is best done just before bedtime.

Forgetting, as such, is not wholly a disadvantage. The tendency to forget should therefore not be regarded as a weakness.

Many things that you acquire by learning have only a temporary value for you. If you were to retain perfectly everything that you learned, those things would constantly be bobbing up and interfering with your adjustment to new situations.

New learning makes it difficult to remember what has been learned in the past, and remembering what has been learned in the past makes it difficult to learn anything new. So you can see how interference works both ways.

Understanding the principle of interference, you can see how valuable it is to forget—when you have to remember.

Forgetting the unimportant helps you remember the important.

Eliminating the clutter helps you accumulate the ideas.

The fact that meaningful material—that is, the material you want and need to remember—is forgotten more slowly than nonsense, simplifies the process for you.

WHAT ABOUT CRAMMING?

There is no moral argument against cramming. The principles of forgetting and remembering are brought into full play in the practice of cramming.

Cramming is done only if you require to know something for a single time; if there will never be any further use for the material learned; if remembering it would be useless—beyond the one time for which it has been crammed into your brain.

Material that has been thoroughly learned disappears from memory more slowly than material that has been just barely learned. That is what cramming is—barely learning a subject or topic. It will be available for your memory the one time you need it and then will conveniently disappear almost completely. Cramming will not interfere with your power of remembering further material—it aids selective forgetting.

Remembering too much can be a curse, as it was to the man who complained about his wife's memory.

"Oh?" said his friend. "Does she forget everything?"

"No," replied the man, "she remembers everything."

Of course, this was probably the man for whom the postmaster at Hastings, Nebraska, had the following sign placed over the letter slots in the post office:

"Have you mailed your wife's letter?"

There are times when it is necessary to remember something for just the next day—like the points of your speech at a sales meeting or at the P.T.A. luncheon. That's just as long as you want to remember it—and you don't want to have it crowding up your memory after you are through with it.

But even if you are making a speech that you may want to forget as soon as it's delivered, you have other considerations, too. You must not forget, as did a former governor, where you are speaking. It seems he forgot who his audience was one day—when he was addressing the convicts at a penitentiary.

He started his address:

"Fellow citizens . . ."

There was a murmur of delight in the auditorium. Confused, the governor started again:

"Fellow convicts . . ."

This drew greater laughter.

"Oh, you know what I mean," he managed to stammer out. "I'm so glad to see so many of you here . . ."

FORGETTING HAS A VALUE _____

It may be an apocryphal story but they say that the governor in question remarked some time later that he had decided to train his memory.

Asked the reason for his decision, he is reported to have said:

"I'm looking for a system that will enable me, when I am interviewed, to remember what to forget."

It is often important to be able to forget. Yet despite this importance, I am sure that you have often blamed yourself for a lapse of memory. Or perhaps you have decried the fact that you too easily forget ideas, plans, and experiences.

It would be unfortunate if you were constantly recalling an infinite number of detailed memories or previous events. You could not carry on any effective thinking if, on seeing a book, for example, you were to recall all that you had read within it.

It would be just as cluttersome if every time you met a friend, you remembered every previous conversation with that person. Or if when you sat down to breakfast each morning you remembered every breakfast you had eaten in the past.

The selective aspect of your memory is one of its greatest strengths. So long as you are capable of remembering *necessary* things, you have established a working base for memory.

It is this selectiveness that perhaps makes people what is commonly called "absent-minded." One philosophy professor was said to have spent an evening with a colleague and his wife. The conversation was spirited until the wee morning hours. After a few yawns went unnoticed, the friend said:

"I hate to put you out, but I have a nine-o'clock class to teach in the morning."

"Oh, dear," said the first professor blushing, "I thought *you* were at *my* house."

You can be certain though that this professor was never absent-minded about his work. It is the absorption in one's own work that may tend to make one an absent-minded forgetter.

PURPOSIVE FORGETTING _____

As Freud did point out, it is often strange how you can remember those things you *want* to remember and forget those things you *want* to forget.

A letter must be sent to confirm an appointment; yet you forget to send it. Were you so busy that you did not have time to put it in the post-office box? And, if you were so busy, why did you remember to send off that note—the same day—accepting a weekend invitation?

There is a psychological reason for this, but such mental blocks are perhaps best not discussed here.

The amount of interest you have in what you are doing is going to help determine your power of successful remembering.

Learning not to forget is largely a matter of learning to find interest in the things you have been prone to forget.

Learning to forget is largely a matter of learning that there are uninteresting things that should be forgotten.

To forget with purpose is to remember with success.

To remember with success is to make your power of remembering a potent force.

Remember:

Purposive forgetting is the key to complete remembering.

Don't clutter up your mind with unimportant things.

Forget them, and you will remember successfully.

MEMORY METER

%	
100%	Remembering Selectively
90%	Recitation
80%	Bird's-Eye View
70%	Spacing Speedup
60%	Reward Giving
50%	Goal Setting
40%	Mental Hooks
30%	Mood Mastery
20%	Memory Motive
10%	Normal Usage

PART THREE

A BONUS

A man's real possession is his memory.
Alexander Smith: *Dreamthorp*.

12

IS THERE "PHOTOGRAPHIC MEMORY"?

Memory: what wonders it performs.
Plutarch: *Morals.*

Of all the things I inherited, why couldn't I have inherited my father's photographic memory?" a student posed to me sadly one day.

It seems that this young woman's father had an excellently trained memory and the family had always labelled it a "photographic memory." Erroneously, I must add; not only in this particular case—but in any case.

There is no such thing as a photographic memory!

There are no people—no matter what their claim may be—who can look at a printed page and be able to reproduce it "photographically." There are no people who can glance at large groups of pictures and tell exactly everything that is in them and where these things are in relation to everything else.

WELL-DEVELOPED MEMORY POWERS _____

Certainly there are people whose memories have been well trained—who make full use of their power to remember. These are the people who have developed *memory-efficiency*. These are people who have learned all the steps to increasing their memory to the hundred-per-cent successful stage. They know all the steps in remembering successfully—and do so.

But to think that the brain is capable of taking impressions in at a glance and retaining them completely and perfectly as if it were a piece of photographic film is erroneous—with one exception: in young children. But I will discuss that with you later.

If you believe that any person who has a successful memory possesses "photographic" ability, you believe a most incredible thing. Ask any person who claims to have a "photographic memory" to look at a page in a telephone book and then recite everything on that page—it can't be done unless the page is carefully studied and the basic principles of remembering as you have learned them in this book are applied.

The idea of the "photographic memory" has grown through the years by misunderstanding of the principles of remembering and misuse of the term "photographic." To the average person who sees a memory feat performed, the only possible explanation seems to be that the performer has a "photographic memory."

There are people who make a profession of demonstrating their memory ability. They will look at a calendar for any year, study it for a few moments, and then be able to tell you the day upon which any date in that year will fall. They can shuffle through a deck of playing cards and name the order of the cards immediately afterward.

This is all done by memory-trickery. It is based on the same association method about which you read in Chapter 5, "MAKE IT MEANINGFUL," and that you now should be utilizing to its fullest extent.

These performers, however, use an association list of anywhere from three hundred to several thousand words. It takes the average "memorologist" several years to master this code list so that it can be used to perform feats of so-called photographic memory.

But it is only trickery, for there is no such thing as a camera mind. It has to be worked at for many years—and, of course, it pays off for the person who is interested in doing such an act in show business.

VIVID VISUAL IMAGES

There are people who are said to have vivid visual images. This vivid visual imagery varies greatly from person to person. An attempt was made to link the possibility of such imagery with artistic effort in the field of painting.

Tests were made and questionnaires prepared for a large group of artists. The intention was to find out whether these artists were painting their pictures from a picture they saw in their "mind's eye," and copying it, more or less.

These tests showed that there was no correlation between these visual images and the artist's ability to create. Some artists did admit that they "saw" in their imagination what they were going to paint. Others had no mental picture at all of what they were painting.

Most artists stated that they created on canvas from a verbalized idea of what they intended to paint. There does not seem to be any correlation between visual imagery and any other ability that people may have. It appears to be a peculiarity that some people have and others do not.

WHY ISN'T IT PHOTOGRAPHIC?

"But if there is such a thing as vivid visual imagery, why can it not be said that this phenomenon is that of 'photographic memory'?" asked a lawyer with whom I had been discussing the accuracy of memory in witnesses.

"Because this vivid visual memory is not as accurate as a photograph," I answered. "For example, suppose you look at a picture and you notice all the detail on it with the exception of one particular detail, and suppose I ask you a question about that detail.

"You could not answer my question about a detail you had not noticed and therefore 'learned' in the original picture. If you had a photograph of that picture, you could look back at it and answer the question about that detail.

"That is what a 'photographic memory' would be—if there were such a thing. You could conjure up in your 'mind's eye' the picture as you saw it and observe a detail in it that you had not consciously observed before.

"Unless you have learned about that detail, unless you have placed it in the visual picture, you cannot answer a question about it. So you see that vivid visual imagery is not as complete as a photograph will be—it never can be unless special effort is made to study every single detail so that you can reproduce it as will."

People who have claimed to have "photographic memory" or who have been acclaimed as having such a gift have been studied under controlled laboratory conditions. The results show that these people do not have photographic memory as such. They cannot answer questions about things they haven't noticed.

THE PROOF IS POSITIVE

Tests have been devised to show that the memory is not photographic. One such interesting test is called the letter square:

```
P L R Z Q
J F X B U
T M V G Y
S W C I K
D N O H E
```

Subjects look at the square for a minute. They then shut their eyes and recall a picture of the square in their mind's eye. Most persons are sure they can do this.

You may be interested; why not try it.

Time yourself carefully. Look at the square for one minute. Then turn the page and answer the questions without again looking at the square, just seeing it in your mind's eye.

1. Repeat the letters of the square.
2. Now repeat them starting at the upper righthand corner and reading them down vertically.
3. Now start at the lower righthand corner and read the lines diagonally up toward the upper lefthand corner.
4. Now start at the lower righthand corner and read the lines right to left and upward to the top.

The first question probably wasn't too difficult to answer.

You most likely repeated the letters from left to right, starting at the top line and moving downward.

But the other three questions undoubtedly gave you a great deal of trouble—as they do everyone, including those who have so-called photographic memories.

Another test involves the use of a list of words. They are everyday words and these well-trained people can remember the list fairly quickly. But when they are asked to spell the words *backward,* they falter badly.

Yet, had these people been able to visualize the list as though it were a photograph in the "mind's eye," they would easily have been able to see the letters in reverse order and spell them. But in fact the image of the list of words is not so clear in their mind that they can see them and recite what they see.

REMEMBERING WHAT YOU WANT _____

The tests showed that people could utilize their power to remember only in those areas that had been set out for remembering. For example, when asked to remember word pairs, the subjects were able to repeat these two-word groups with some facility. But if asked, without warning, to name the second word in each pair, they found it quite difficult.

Another example proving that successful remembering is not a photographic process is that of showing the subjects words each of which is on a different card. The cards are of different colors. The subjects will be able to recall the words, but when asked—without previous warning that this was to be noticed or remembered—the color of the card for each specific word, they will be unable to remember this.

So you see that under laboratory conditions this so-called photographic memory breaks down. The memory cannot behave like a camera, suddenly sighting something and instantaneously remembering it.

There is no beautiful photograph that comes effortlessly to the "mind's eye" to help anyone in perfecting a successful memory.

Memory for anyone does not come effortlessly. Remembering embodies all of the steps you have learned in the previous chapters.

EIDETIC IMAGES _____

As I pointed out earlier, there is a partial exception to the fact that "photographic memory" does not exist.

Some children have a very strong and immediate image after seeing something. It is an after-image much the same as the memory echo which I discussed in Chapter 8, "THE SPACING SPEEDUP."

These children, usually before they reach their teens, can look at something and actually see it almost as a photograph for a short time after they originally view it.

Although this is a strong image, it is not identical to the original thing they viewed. It has been found to be warped and changed and molded by their interests. If they find something in what they are shown that particularly interests them, they will see it as larger than it was. Or it may be interpreted differently, according to the interests and ideas of the particular child.

The echo—called an *eidetic image*—remains only for a few seconds after the child has looked at something. It is not (as a "photographic memory" is supposed to be) a permanent memory.

This eidetic image, known by psychologists also as a *primary memory image,* is a phenomenon most common in later childhood; it fades out during adolescence.

Eidetic imagery will help a child answer a question about something seen a moment before even though the child did not view the object or picture with any special interest. But instead of being completely photographic, the memory is somewhat plastic: objects may change size, things may move, color may vary in intensity and hue—and all changes are either voluntary or involuntary, usually modified by the child's particular interests.

With the minor exception, then, of eidetic imagery in children, there is no such thing as "photographic memory."

13

HOW TO HELP YOUR CHILDREN

Memory is the mother of all wisdom.
Aeschylus: *Prometheus Bound.*

The business of learning is one of the most important in the life of every person.

It starts off in childhood as the most important thing. At all levels of education—primary, secondary, and in college—it is a vital process to the child. But it is just as important later in life. It is important to the adult—in business and at home.

Parents have often asked how they can help their children learn more effectively.

HELP YOURSELF, TOO

With this problem in mind—together with the problem that learning sometimes is an insurmountable chore for adults—this chapter was conceived. It is designed to help you help your child. It also is designed to help you help yourself.

In the second section of this book you learned the secrets of using your power to remember—and using it successfully. Now you have the opportunity of further cementing this knowledge within your own memory by helping your child to acquire it.

The best way to start to learn anything that has to be learned—whether it is a lesson in school, or a principle of interior decorating, or a formula for profit based on production—is to make practical use of what you are learning.

By helping your child and in this way using your knowledge in a practical manner, you are making sure that the secrets of a more powerful and successful memory remain with you.

You remember how in your own work as a student you constantly found it necessary to recall specific facts, the exact wording of formulas, the sequence of arguments, passages of poetry or prose, and other such information. This remembering was in many ways identical to the remembering you now have to do in everyday living: people's names and faces, facts and outcomes of conferences, points and figures for sales arguments, intricate directions or instructions, and similar material.

INCREASING THE MEMORY POWER _____

In the preceding pages, you have learned how to increase the power of remembering successfully. Now you have the opportunity to help your children do the same thing, and to help them use this power advantageously in their work at school.

How can you utilize what you have learned in this book to help your children?

The process of memory consists in learning, retaining, and recalling. But there are other primary factors involved. The first of these is motivation.

What is the motive for your children's learning? The answer is obvious, of course. But your children must be made to understand *why* it is important to have an education, what an education can mean to their future, and how the groundwork for this education depends on their using the power of remembering to its utmost.

Make your children realize that in studying any subject, they are better off doing so with the help of someone else who is interested in that subject.

If you want to learn a new subject, you know how you are going to seek friends who have an active interest in that subject. In this way the material you are learning will be used in discussion and remain with you more firmly.

The same applies to students. If it is history that your children seem to have difficulty understanding and remembering, then have them find students who have a keen interest in this subject. This will stimulate your children's sense of competition and the ensuing discussions of history will help their memories.

Setting of a definite goal, which you realize is so valuable to you in learning new work, has the same value to your children. The goal is, of course, mastery of the subject at the particular level it is being taught so that examination can be written and passed.

DAYDREAMERS

Children, like adults, are prone to moodiness. Many factors contribute to a child's being unwilling to study: outside distractions, outside influences, physiological changes.

These factors are the moods that have to be mastered, as in your own case.

Children who in adolescence day dream about a girl friend or a boy friend are distracted from the task at hand: studying.

Children who see playmates and schoolmates who appear never to study yet still do well will feel they can do the same.

Children who try to keep up with what is going on in the world of radio or television will insist that they can study just as easily with the radio or TV set playing as with it turned off.

The distraction of radio or television is a great problem to many parents. They see that their children are managing to do homework despite the set's being turned on, and so they are falsely convinced that this practice may continue without doing any harm.

DISTRACTION COSTS ENERGY

The fact that your children can manage to do homework while listening to or watching their favorite programs does not mean that they are not being distracted from doing better work more efficiently.

It has been proved that such distraction is costly in the process of learning. The remembering process is a spender of bodily energy—just like any other process. So is the listening process. If your children are doing two things at once, the remembering process loses the energy that must be spent in overcoming the distraction. They tire more easily because their expenditure of bodily energy is increased.

To learn successfully, to remember successfully, you must devote all your energy to the task at hand.

Of course, although the expending of energy in the performance of two tasks at the same time can interfere with the success of learning and studying, the brain itself cannot tire from overstudying.

You remember that experiment has proved the brain does not fatigue even after extreme effort. The fatigue your children may complain of after studying for a length of time may be the result of working against distraction or may only be an excuse to escape from the situation of doing homework.

Genuine fatigue is possible—the physical fatigue of working in a position that is entirely uncomfortable. Fatigue will increase if the proper conditions do not exist for comfortable studying.

Of course, comfort cannot be too great. Comfort has not been found to be an aid to successful remembering—that is, comfort of the "favorite armchair" variety. This type of comfort is conducive only to relaxation. Relaxation reduces the desire to work; and thus it becomes easy to wander off mentally from the task at hand.

A good, comfortable posture chair is the answer. Too much discomfort can be just as distracting as too much comfort. A chair that does not permit too great relaxation will keep the body's muscles in a position of slight tension and this, as you remember, contributes to efficiency of learning.

But, remember, the brain will not tire.

TRICKS OF REMEMBERING

The use of "meaning" in the practice of studying is an important one. The more meaningful the material being learned, the more likely it is to be memorized—and the longer it will be remembered.

Even if certain material has to be learned by rote, you have learned earlier how by adding meaning to it, the process of remembering can be speeded up and the memory-efficiency made stronger.

Help your children to understand the processes of association: connection with known material, puns, mnemonic devices, vividness, tricks of grouping and adding rhythm as has been outlined in Chapter 5, "MAKE IT MEANINGFUL."

Memorizing lists of words in French, or Spanish, or German, can be greatly aided by such methods. Learning formulas or rules can be greatly simplified by utilizing the tricks of memory.

What can you do to reward your children after their homework has been finished? Even if your children are not unwilling to sit down daily and do the work set by their teachers, a reward upon completion of homework is a good incentive at all times.

Are there special desserts that they like? Phone calls to friends? Television programs they like to watch? Short games? A chat with parents? Perhaps, some candy or fruit? No matter what it is, it can be the reward for homework completed and well done.

NINE STEPS TO ECONOMY

Proper management of conditions of efficient learning will give your children an economy in memorizing that will make the daily task of homework a quicker and more efficient one.

Here are nine steps to effecting such economy.

1. The complete effort of the time set aside for homework must be directed toward that task and that task only.

2. Memorizing is made more efficient if your children can discover the meaning of the material they are to learn. This is an important task for you—helping your children find meaning in what they are learning.

3. Reviewing improves the memory and reduces the process of forgetting. It also produces "overlearning."

4. Memorizing by spaced repetition will save time in the overall learning. Massed repetition is a time-waster.

5. The "whole" method is preferable as a time-saver to the "part" method.

6. Purposeful forgetting is valuable in helping to avoid a cluttered mind.

7. Cramming has the value of helping students study for examinations in subjects that will have little value to them in later life. It must not, however, be encouraged for all examinations and for all study. It is a short-cut to memorizing: but an education is of greatest value when the whole route is travelled.

8. Interference is a waste of time, energy, and effort. Studies should be done with a minimum opportunity for interference. Space subjects so that no two similar ones are studied one following the other. In other words, don't have French homework follow Spanish homework, but have some other non-similar subject be studied between them.

*9. The most important rule of economy in studying is recita-
tion. It provides greatest retention of what is learned. Have
your children close their textbooks and recite to you, if possible, while you check them. Or encourage them to study with
friends so they may recite to each other, provided they don't
distract each other.*

Individuals differ in memory ability. But any person can
improve remembering by better management and better method of
memory. Practice, provided all the proper techniques are used, is
effective in improving the process of memorizing.

MAKING AND USING NOTES

Especially in college, good notes that are well made, well kept, and
properly used, constitute a tool of memory of the highest value.

Almost any job can be made easier by the use of notes. Almost any job can be done better by using notes. And some
jobs—such as writing term papers—cannot be done at all without
proper organization of material and proper note-taking.

One of the best things any student can do is to acquire the
skill of taking and using notes. It is a skill that will come into greater
and greater usage in later life, as you yourself can easily prove to
your children.

What are good notes? What makes them good?

The answer is simply this: Good notes are those that help
your power to remember successfully. Their purpose is to help the
mind do a good job of thinking. By keeping a comprehensive set of
notes, your children will have at their fingertips all the facts they require in reviewing for examinations and for writing papers.

There are three principles in taking notes.

*1. There is the ability to make notes that will give a practical
and usable record of what the student has read.
2. The same type of record has to be made of everything the
student hears in the classroom lecture.
3. Notes can be valuable in keeping a complete record of the
student's own ideas and thoughts.*

Why should notes be made from reading matter? "After all,"
one student once challenged me, "the material is already written in
a book, all I have to do is look it up again." Very true—but what an

uneconomical way of reviewing and refreshing the memory and what a waste of time in regathering material for a paper to be written.

DECIDE WHAT IS IMPORTANT _____

In making notes from books, it is necessary to keep an open eye for those things that are important and that summarize the themes of the work. It may slow you down, certainly, but it has two advantages: first, it provides a readily available record of the facts; second, it helps impress on the memory since it acts much like recitation.

To be practical about taking notes, the student must have clearly in mind what purposes the notes are for. Certainly it is silly to take notes for a term paper on material that will not be required. It is just as silly to make reference notes that will be of no value in studying for an examination.

What then should be included in notes? What should be omitted?

In determining this the student has to ask three questions:

1. *Can these notes be used for study, or review, or writing a paper?*
2. *Can this work be done by referring only to the notes, or must the original material be referred to again?*
3. *Can this work be done at some date later than that on which the notes were made?*

If the answer to any of the above questions is not "yes," then the notes are of no great value to the student.

The final rule on note-taking when reading is: *Don't make a note until you have read through the passage once.* In that way you are sure of taking notes of material you need.

NOTES FROM CLASS _____

Good students do not merely assimilate what the teacher says. They allow it to turn over in their minds, mix it with their own ideas and thoughts, develop reactions to it, and in that way make it a part of themselves.

Notes from classroom lectures and discussion must be captured for later and more leisurely consideration. The question to be answered in this regard is: What should be written down?

The answer varies, of course, with the instructor. Some teach around the outskirts of a subject with the hope of encouraging students to have an interest and dig deeply into it themselves. Others insist on talking at a slow rate and demand that every word be taken down. There are other variations between these two approaches to instruction.

The first thing the student has to do is to get an idea of how the instructor uses classroom time. If a survey of the course is distributed at the start of the semester, the note-taking will be built around this outline. If not, an outline has to be determined from the lecturer's general pattern of procedure; and the notes should round that pattern out.

Everything should be organized under topical headings so that later when the student brings together the notes, rhyme and reason will appear.

An important phase of classroom note-taking is watching for comments, interpretations, and evaluations that the instructor will make with regard to various readings. These are helpful in effective independent study because they give students the slant they need.

A TYPICAL SET OF NOTES _____

An example of the organization of notes, preserving the sequence of thought and enhancing the review value, follows:

    I. How habits are broken.
       A. Disuse leads to disappearance. Real problem is how to start the disuse. Habits we desire to break afford satisfaction, therefore:
          1. We cannot rely upon principle of disuse.
          2. Nor upon "willing" or wishing to break them.
       B. Must form positive and satisfying counterhabits.
          1. To break nail-biting, manicure and polish nails; take an active pride in appearance of hands.
          2. Practice art of being good company to overcome grouchiness.
             a. Greater skill, at first, as a grouch than as a pleasant person.

      b. *But ambition plus practice of being good company breaks habits of grouchiness.*
   C. *If annoyance accompanies the habit, then practice the habit intentionally.*
      1. *Illustration of the principle:*
         a. *When "hte" is written on the typewriter for "the," force yourself in practice to write "hte" but always with the intention not to repeat the error in future typing.*
         b. *If one stammers, then stammer intentionally and as nearly as possible like involuntary stammering.*
         c. *Nail-biting might be overcome by deliberate performance and with the thought that in future the act will be performed voluntarily.*
      2. *Explanation of the principle:*
         a. *Extinction of conditioned reflex requires that the sound of a bell not be followed by feeding. Absence of feeding eliminates the habit of secreting saliva at sound of bell.*
         b. *If you write "hte" for "the," then a check-up breaks the habit.*
         c. *By intentional repetition the habit is not repeated exactly.*
            i. *Difference in motivation.*
            ii. *Difference in outcome. The check-up deprives habit of its fascination.*

THE STUDENT'S OWN IDEAS

Some people carry notebooks with them at all times so that they can make a record of anything they feel may be useful to them at a later date.

From time to time, they go through their notes to see what their reactions are and how they can use anything they have recorded previously.

Such notes can be used by students to list interpretations or criticisms that occur to them during their work. They can be used to record ideas in general, or possible examination questions, or topics for term papers, or questions about things they do not understand, or problems that have been puzzling.

They are the starting point for further mental work. Many

ideas pass through the mind from time to time, but they are only interferences to the work being done at the time and as such are most likely to be forgotten.

The notebook, then, is the best method for capturing these thoughts so that they can be reviewed at a more appropriate time and be made use of.

Personal note-taking is of great value in the study of foreign languages. Vocabulary and grammatical constructions that the student finds unfamiliar should be noted. It is best to list such words and phrases in sentences so that they have meaning rather than just being a list.

Notes are more than mechanical records. They are working tools in the application of remembering and thinking.

WHAT ABOUT EXAMINATIONS

Examinations are often a source of worry to most students. But they have a great value in the process of education and they must be faced in a practical manner.

Some students seem to feel that they can disregard their daily work and can, by vigorously cramming at the end, make up for the neglect and pass the exam. This is a dangerous attitude. It can work with certain types of subject matter, certain students or certain teachers, but it is a treacherous course to follow as a general practice.

The worst aspect is that subjects so studied are not going to be retained. Most everything that is taught in lower schools and everything learned in higher education courses should be remembered. It is needed as a basis for further studies. Cramming, as you have seen already, is only for today—*when tomorrow isn't necessary.*

Good cramming, of course, will serve as a review to students who have done their work all term. Review shortly before an examination serves the memory by providing repetition and recency—conditions favorable to recall.

How, then, should your children prepare for an examination?

Most important is to be physically fit. A good night's sleep is important as it provides a rested body. A light meal before taking the examination is important because the mental processes can be retarded if a heavy meal is eaten.

When the student gets the examination paper, the questions should be surveyed carefully. The whole paper should be looked at before the writing begins. Then each question should be carefully read to discover just what is required.

Too often students read into a test question what they *think* is being asked, and write the wrong answer.

While writing answers, students should make note of passing ideas that don't belong at the point they are writing about at the moment. Too often these ideas are good ones but are forgotten when the appropriate place is reached.

Planning of the time set for the writing of the test should be done so that too much time isn't given to one section and consequently not enough time left for other portions.

Waiting for inspiration is a waste of time for students. Rather than doing nothing until the right idea comes to mind they should start to write. As they begin to explore the subject and express their knowledge, one idea will help the recall of another and eventually what was being sought will be remembered.

Even after their student days, your children may have to write examinations. They may be candidates for state or city licenses as physicians, dentists, lawyers, barbers, or certified public accountants, or they may seek Civil Service positions.

The intelligent approach to examination writing is as important in the examination as the remembering of the required facts.

14

HOW TO REMEMBER ANECDOTES AND SPEECHES

Memory is the diary that we all carry about with us.
Oscar Wilde.

Most of us, at some time or another, are faced with the prospect of telling—or wanting to tell—a humorous story.

Unfortunately, too often we don't tell it, tell it in slightly butchered fashion, or get someone else who knows the story to tell it.

"I just can't tell a story," is an excuse that is often heard, "because I never recall the details and usually forget the punch line."

Well, if that's the case, better not to tell it. There's nothing worse than a good story poorly told.

The story, whether told by itself simply for the sake of relating an anecdote or as part of a speech, can be extremely important. It helps to color our everyday conversation with bright spots, it is of value in bridging awkward gaps in conversations, and is the usual forerunner to any speech—short or long—so that an audience can be placed in a listening frame of mind quickly.

"Oh," you may say, "I never need to worry about making a speech. Such things just don't occur in my life."

Well, that may have been so up to now—or maybe you have already passed up such opportunities because you felt you could not construct and remember a speech.

SPEECHES, SHORT OR LONG

Speeches may be required of you at social gatherings celebrating weddings, birthdays, or anniversaries. You may be attending a business meeting and have to express your viewpoint on a certain problem. Or you may be at a political gathering and feel that you have something to contribute to the discussion.

Sometimes it may take days or weeks to prepare yourself for such a speech. At other times you may have only a few minutes to prepare yourself for a talk, or you may even have to talk on the spur of the moment.

In any case, it is necessary that you be able to express yourself clearly and without fear. It is vital that you are able to face an audience—whether it is comprised of friends and relatives, or of business associates who may or may not be entirely in sympathy with you.

Being able to stand on your feet and talk to a group of people or being forced to refuse because you feel that you are unable to express yourself in front of others can easily mean the difference between success and failure in your life.

If you are going to be a wallflower and creep into a quiet corner because you are unwilling to face the spotlight and accept the attention that is due to you, the chances are that few people are going to be interested enough in you to try and bring you out of it.

You may be a master in your own particular field. You may have in a corner of your brain the secret of overcoming some everyday problem that will be a boon to mankind. But what good will it do if you cannot talk about it, fight for it—by talking intelligently and holding the attention of those to whom you are talking.

THE VALUE OF THE ANECDOTE

It was Abraham Lincoln who summarized the value of a story so well. He said:

"They say I tell a great many stories; I reckon I do.

"But I have found in the course of a long experience that

common people, take them as they run, are more easily informed through the medium of a broad illustration than in any other way."

There was a speechmaker whose words have lived. He knew how to talk to the occasion. When a story would serve a purpose, he used one.

But how to remember stories?

Well, here are some taken from a collection of anecdotes and quotations.

Read them through and see if you cannot retell them after a single reading.

"Alert?" repeated a member of Congress when questioned concerning a political opponent.

"Why he's as alert as a Providence bridegroom I heard of the other day. You know how bridegrooms, starting off on their honeymoons, sometimes forget all about their brides and buy tickets only for themselves?

"That is what happened to the Providence young man. And when his wife said to him, 'Why, Tom, you bought only one ticket!' he answered without a moment's hesitation, 'By Jove, you're right dear—I'd forgotten about myself entirely!' "

A man lost a valuable dog and advertised in the local newspaper offering five hundred dollars for it, but got no replies. He called at the newspaper office.

"I want to see the advertising manager," he said.

"He's out," said the office boy.

"Well, how about his assistant?"

"He's out too, sir."

"Then I'll see the city editor."

"He's out, sir."

"What about the managing editor?"

"He's also out, sir."

"Goodness! Is everybody out?"

"Yes sir—they're all hunting for your dog."

When Champ Clark was speaker of the House, Congressman Johnson of Indiana interrupted the speech of an Ohio representative, calling him a jackass.

The expression was ruled unparliamentary and Johnson apologized.

"I withdraw the unfortunate word, Mr. Speaker, but I insist that the gentleman from Ohio is out of order."

"How am I out of order?" angrily shouted the Ohio congressman.

"Probably a veterinary could tell you," answered Johnson.

And this was allowed to enter the record.

A young woman, interested in writing, met a noted author at a party.

"I wonder if you can help me out?" she asked. "Tell me how many words there are in a novel."

The author was taken aback, but managed a sympathetic smile.

"Well, that depends," he said. "A short novel would run about 65,000 words."

"You mean 65,000 words make a novel?"

"Yes," he said hesitatingly. "More or less."

"Well, how do you like that!" shouted the woman gleefully. "My book is finished!"

Late one stormy night a physician was aroused from sleep by a farmer who lived several miles out in the country. The farmer, who had the reputation of being "a little near," first inquired how much the doctor charged for country calls.

"Fifteen dollars," snapped the doctor, impatient that the fellow would bargain under such circumstances.

Thereupon the farmer urged the doctor to drive him home immediately. So the doctor dressed and drove the farmer to his house with as much speed as the muddy, slippery roads permitted.

As soon as they stopped in front of the farmer's house, the farmer stepped from the automobile, took fifteen dollars from his pocket and handed them to the doctor.

"But where is the patient?" demanded the doctor.

"There ain't none," answered the country man, "but that there livery man would have charged me twenty-five dollars to bring me out here tonight."

A Georgia cracker sitting, ragged and barefoot, on the steps of his tumbledown shack, was accosted by a stranger who stopped for a drink of water.

Wishing to be agreeable, the stranger said, "How is your cotton coming on?"

"Ain't got none," the farmer said.

"Didn't you plant any?" asked the stranger.

"Nope," said the cracker, " 'fraid of boll weevils."

"Well," said the stranger, "how is your corn?"

"Didn't plant none. 'Fraid there wasn't going to be no rain."

The stranger, confused but persevering, added, "Well, how are your potatoes?"

"Ain't gone none. Scairt o' potato bugs."

"Really; what did you plant?" asked the astonished visitor.

"Nothin'," answered the cracker. "I jes' played it safe."

"Did I understand you to say that this boy voluntarily confessed his share in the mischief done to the schoolhouse?" asked the judge, addressing the determined-looking female parent of a small and dirty boy who was charged with having been concerned in a recent raid upon an unpopular schoolmaster.

"Yes, sir, he did," the woman responded. "I just had to persuade him a little and then he told the whole thing voluntarily."

"How did you persuade him?" inquired the judge.

"Well, first I gave him a good licking," said the firm parent, "and then I put him right to bed without any supper and I took all his clothes away and I told him he's to stay in bed till he told me what he'd done, if 'twas the rest of his days, and I should lick him again in the morning.

"And in less than half an hour, sir, he told me the whole story voluntarily."

Some years ago, Notre Dame's star football center, Frankie Szymanski, appeared in a South Bend court as a witness in a civil suit.

"Are you on the Notre Dame football team this year?" asked the judge.

"Yes, your Honor."

"What position?"

"Center, your Honor."

"How good a center?"

Szymanski squirmed in his chair, but in confident tones admitted, "Sir, I'm the best center Notre Dame ever had."

Coach Frank Leahy, who was in the courtroom, was surprised because the lad had always been modest and unassuming.

When proceedings were adjourned, the coach asked him why he had made such a statement.

Szymanski blushed.

"I hated to do it, coach," he explained, "but, after all, I was under oath."

Dwight L. Moody, the great evangelist, was calling with a certain minister on a wealthy lady, to ask her help in a building operation.

On the way over, Moody asked the minister what sum he had in mind.

"Oh," said the pastor, "perhaps $1,000."

"Better let me handle the matter," suggested the evangelist.

"Madam," said Moody, after the usual introduction, "we have come to ask you for $5,000 toward the building of a new Mission."

The lady threw up her hands in horror.

"Oh, Mr. Moody!" she exclaimed, "I couldn't possibly give more than $3,000."

And the pair walked away with a check for just that sum.

A peddler of lottery tickets tried to sell a chance to Baron Rothschild, head of the famous European banking family.

"What would I want with a lottery ticket?" protested the annoyed Baron.

"Oh, come on," pleaded the peddler. "They're only fifty cents each. Go on, take a chance."

In order to get rid of the nuisance, Baron Rothschild bought the lottery ticket. The next day, bright and early, the peddler was back on the Baron's doorstep.

"You won first prize!" he cried. "$300,000!"

"Well," exclaimed the pleased Baron. "I suppose I ought to reward you."

He thought for a moment and then asked:

"Which would you rather have—$12,000 in cash or $3,600 a year for the rest of your life?"

"Give me the $12,000," said the peddler. "With the kind of luck you Rothschilds have, I wouldn't live another six months."

HOW TO REMEMBER THEM _____

You have read the ten anecdotes through once. How many do you think you remember?

Take a pencil and in the following space write one sentence that will give the idea of each story. I have summarized the first story to give you an idea of how you can summarize the others.

1. *Alertness of a forgetful bridegroom who told his bride he had forgotten to buy a honeymoon ticket for himself, not her.*

2. _____

3. _____

4. _____

5. _____

6. _____

7. _____

8. _____

9. _____

10. _____

Did you remember the essence of all ten stories? Chances are you did not. If you had been told them one at a time over a period of days, or even several hours, you may have had better results.

You are inclined to listen to a humorous story, laugh at it, and promptly forget it. But such stories can help to make you a successful person in your association with people in all walks of life.

How, then, are you going to help yourself to remember stories?

The first of the memory rules to apply to material of this sort is that of making it meaningful.

USING YOUR MENTAL HOOKS _____

You already have a set of ten mental hooks which you should be using for short lists, just as this group of stories proves to be.

Let us see how this Mental Hook List can be brought into play here, remembering that vividness is a help to memory.

1. *Me*—picture yourself in the ludicrous position of having only bought one railway ticket for two people and, therefore, having to get off the train and walk the rest of the way yourself.

2. *Shoe*—the lost dog has run off with your shoe and everyone looking for it is forced to do so with one shoe off.

3. *Kittens*—Your kitten has become ill and you have taken it to the veterinary where, while waiting, it begins to talk and tells you the story of a member of Congress who implied another was a jackass.

4. *Table*—On a table is a huge pile of papers with markers setting off every two hundred pages each of which is marked "one novel—65,000 words."

5. *Fingers*—Picture yourself standing in the rain to pay the doctor and the money sticks to your fingers so that no matter how hard you try you can only pay fifteen dollars.

6. *Sticks*—In a farm field there are row upon row of sticks set in the ground to hold up new plants, but when you look at the paper markers at the head of each row on each is written the word: "nothing."

7. *Dice*—A woman is playing dice with her son. He keeps on winning and begs his mother to allow him to tell her voluntarily that he had "loaded" the dice so that he could win, but she refuses to allow him to tell her of his crimes.

8. *Gate*—A witness in the courtroom is being questioned by the judge and swings back and forth on the gate to the witness box while tossing a football at the judge.

9. *Baseball*—A woman playing baseball at a church picnic hits the ball into the outfield; it is caught by the pastor and disintegrates into hundred-dollar bills—at first ten of them and then suddenly twenty more to total $3,000.

10. *Indians*—A tribe of Indians perform a war dance around a prisoner who turns out to be Baron Rothschild and he offers them money to let him go; they take it because they decide he's too lucky to remain captured.

OTHER MEANS OF REMEMBERING STORIES _____

The Mental Hook List is but one way to remember a group of stories.
Suppose you use the system of making a memory chain.

Let us look back at the stories and see if we can pick out key words to associate with each and then tie them into a chain. The key words might easily be these:

1. *wedding*
2. *lost dog*
3. *jackass*
4. *novel*
5. *doctor*
6. *farmer*
7. *schoolboy*
8. *courtroom*
9. *church*
10. *lottery*

Now by linking these key words together what sort of chain might we be able to make so that the ten stories will remain in our memories?

If I were doing this, here is the sort of chain I might construct:

church   *(9)*

                    visualize a wedding taking place in a church

wedding   *(1)*

                    the person getting married is a doctor

doctor   *(5)*

                    the best man is a farmer

farmer   *(6)*

                    the farmer leaves riding a jackass

jackass   *(3)*

                    to look for his lost dog

lost dog   *(2)*

        he finds the dog in the arms of a schoolboy

schoolboy   *(7)*

        who is in a courtroom

courtroom   *(8)*

        *where he has just been informed he has won
        a lottery*

lottery   *(10)*

        the prize being a copy of a new novel

novel   *(4)*

At first try to repeat the chain. Then, with the help of the key words, repeat the ten anecdotes. Try again next week; then next month. You will be surprised to learn how quickly such a chain can be firmly established in your memory.

PREPARING SPEECHES

Your ability to use your memory successfully is going to be a great boon in speech-making.

Nothing is more disconcerting to the people to whom you have to speak than the use of a written text which you half read and half stumble through in trying to find your place.

A former U.S. Ambassador was one speaker who realized how valuable it was to speak "off the cuff." A reporter friend of mine told me that this man would appear on the platform with a piece of paper in his hand.

But as soon as he got up to talk, he would look around the audience and say: "Hello, Jack," "Hello, Tom," and then remark that he hadn't known so many of his friends were going to be in the audience.

"I don't need notes to talk to *you* people," he would say. "To you I can speak from my heart."

Then he would throw away the piece of paper.

My friend, who had covered several meetings at which this happened, decided to check one night to see just what the notes were that the man had tossed aside. So he mounted the platform after the meeting and recovered the piece of paper. It was an old laundry bill.

The contact between speaker and audience, which is most vital for success, is immediately lost if you have to resort to your text, or even to copious notes. The contact you have to establish is done not only through your speech content and the tone of your voice, it is accomplished to a great extent by eye.

That is to say: by looking at your audience directly, you will make all your listeners feel that you are talking specifically to them. This feeling cannot be created by looking at, or reading, your manuscript.

A good speech is a conversation between the speaker and the listeners. By watching your audience you can attune yourself to their reactions. Unlike in personal conversation, your listeners cannot talk back. You, therefore, must be able to tell by looking at them what they may be thinking, and especially when they might become bored, so that you can successfully come to a conclusion without losing any of your earlier effectiveness.

This you can only do if you have mastered your topic. You will find that you will prepare just as carefully to speak without a manuscript as you might if you wanted to read your speech. But to prepare a speech so that you can speak directly to your audience and not use your written manuscript, you have to know your topics thoroughly.

EIGHT STEPS TO PREPARING A SPEECH _____

In brief, here are eight steps you should use in preparing any speech—short or long.

1. Have something of importance to say. Make it specific.
2. Select your major theme or idea and make everything else subordinate to that.
3. Stick to your topic.
4. Research your factual data carefully. Your opinion is your own, but your facts should be absolutely correct.

5. Build an outline: Get a short, sharp introduction (using an anecdote is ideal); build the body of your speech to support your main theme and slant illustrative anecdotes to your audience; hit your climax, summarize your main idea, restate your main point—and stop there. Remember the story of one bored listener who slipped away from a dinner speaker and was joined by a second diner ten minutes later. "Hasn't he finished yet?" asked the first. "He finished a long time ago," the second replied, "he just won't stop."
6. Transcribe the main points of your speech to brief notes.
7. Familiarize yourself with your material, using the chain method.
8. Go back and drop in illustrative anecdotes wherever the speech seems to bog down.

In order to construct your chain of a speech, it is not necessary to write down the entire speech. Writing the entire speech out may lead to the bad habit of learning a speech by heart. And the listener knows quite easily if a speech is memorized word for word, or whether the speaker knows the subject and is speaking more or less extemporaneously.

You must list your main ideas and selected key words so that you have a chain of thought that will immediately give to you the essence of your topic.

In selecting your key words for a speech, they should have two meanings in your mind. They first must recall the thoughts for which they were selected. Second, they must be able to tie together into a chain that will key your memory into presenting the material you need in its logical order.

Before you go further, you must master the chain. Each key word must come easily as soon as the previous one is thought of. There must be no mechanical memorizing: the association of one key word to the next must be clear and simple.

A SPEECH EXAMPLE

Let us look at one of history's most famous speeches and see how we can link up key words with connecting thoughts in preparing ourselves for a speaking assignment.

Lincoln's famous address on the battlefield at Gettysburg is a prime example of how a speech should be constructed. Because of the occasion, Lincoln avoided the use of anecdotes. But he kept his speech short, to the point, and powerful by the avoidance of extraneous words.

Four score and seven years ago our fathers brought forth on this continent, a new nation, conceived in Liberty, and dedicated to the proposition that all men are created equal.

Now we are engaged in a great civil war, testing whether that nation, or any nation so conceived and so dedicated can long endure. We are met on a great battle-field of that war. We have come to dedicate a portion of that field, as a final resting place for those who here gave their lives that that nation might live. It is altogether fitting and proper that we should do this.

But, in a larger sense, we can not dedicate—we can not consecrate—we can not hallow—this ground. The brave men, living and dead, who struggled here, have consecrated it, far above our poor power to add or detract. The world will little note, nor long remember what we say here, but it can never forget what they did here. It is for us the living, rather, to be dedicated here to the unfinished work which they who fought here have thus far so nobly advanced. It is rather for us to be here dedicated to the great task remaining before us—that from these honored dead we take increased devotion to that cause for which they gave the last full measure of devotion—that we here highly resolve that these dead shall not have died in vain—that this nation, under God, shall have a new birth of freedom—and that government of the people, by the people, for the people, shall not perish from the earth.

Let us construct a chain, then, for Lincoln's address and see what it looks like.

Key words	*Linking thought*

Four score and seven years ago

. . . a new nation . . .

	Why?

. . . conceived in Liberty

. . . dedicated to proposition

Key words	Linking thought

. . . *all men are created equal.*

What has happened?

. . . *now engaged in war* . . .

For what reason?

. . . *testing whether such a*

nation can long endure . . .

Why are we here?

. . . *to dedicate a final*

resting place to those who

died . . .

Should this be done?

. . . *it is fitting and*

proper that we do this . . .

But can we do this?

. . . *in a sense, we can not* . . .

Why not?

. . . *for those who have fought*

here have already done so . . .

What can we do, then?

. . . *we must be dedicated*

Key words	Linking thought

here . . .

To what?

. . . to the unfinished work

they started . . .

Which is?

. . . the remaining task . . .

of giving this nation a new

birth of freedom . . .

To what end?

. . . so that government of

the people, by the people, for

the people, shall not perish

from the earth.

In constructing your list of key words, you list only those that have been listed on the left-hand side of the page. The words that were listed on the right-hand side are the connecting thoughts. They have no place in your written preparation. They are only the thoughts which will link you from key to key in the development of your speech.

DELIVERING THE SPEECH

Now that you have mastered the plan of preparation of your speech, you must remember the eight basic rules of delivering a speech.

1. Speak in a natural tone. Do not raise your voice. Your speech is no more than a conversation with a large group of people.

2. Don't stand like a ventriloquist's dummy. Be animated. Let your voice, your expression, your attitude and your bodily movements show that you mean what you say.

3. Nervousness is to be expected, so don't let it throw you. Even the most experienced speakers suffer from nervousness before they start to deliver a talk. Most actors and actresses say that if they ever stopped being nervous before the curtain went up for each performance, they would give up the theatre because they would know they no longer had the ability to act.

4. Choose your words with care. Use strong, but simple, language. Understatement is always more effective than overstatement.

5. Don't forget to look the members of your audience right in the eye.

6. Hecklers should be dealt with calmly and without loss of temper. Deal with distractions from the audience promptly. A story is told of a novelist who was hissed during a public address. Without a moment's hesitation, he said: "Only three things hiss—a goose, a snake, and a fool. Step up and let us identify you!"

7. Speak your speech, don't read it. If you must refer to notes, do so. But don't carry your full manuscript with you—nothing you have to say is worth more time than you can spend on it by delivering it "off the cuff."

8. Keep within your time limit. One successful speaker at-tributed his success to the fact that he talked until he got tired, *while other speakers talked until* the audience *got tired.*

15

USING YOUR MEMORY IN DISCUSSIONS AND CONFERENCES

Reading maketh a full man, conference a ready man.
Francis Bacon: *Of Studies.*

There is nothing as convincing as the facts!

You can be as convincing as you like in your manner or your presentation; if you haven't got the facts to back you up your arguments lack value.

But how to have and retain the facts?

The answer is simply "use your memory."

Facts make the argument. Facts win the discussion. Facts steer the conference.

In the chapters that preceded, you learned how to make the fullest use of your memory. You may ask, "But how can I learn to remember unrelated facts?" You have the answer many times over. They can be keyed to the Mental Hook List. They can be formed into associations. They can be linked into a chain.

No matter what it is you want to remember—so that you can go into a conference or a discussion well armed—you can retain it if you use your memory successfully.

Someone once said to me, "Oh, but I don't participate in discussions or conferences."

Perhaps you feel the same way. Maybe you think that the idea of discussions and conferences is for Big Business.

It's not. Every day, in more ways than you perhaps realize, you participate in just such exchanges of ideas.

Why don't you do, right now, what I asked my friend to do. Take a pencil and in the space below list every telephone conversation you have had today. On the left write the name of the person to whom you spoke; on the right list what the conversation was about:

Person's Name   **Subject**

That was a longer list than you thought, wasn't it?

Now, while you still have the pencil, why not think back to last night and list the topics covered with your family at home:

Topics Discussed at Home

Again, I'm sure you were surprised that you had had so many discussions—yes, I said *discussions.* That is exactly what they are. Every time you have a conversation on the phone, every time you talk to your spouse, the neighbors, your friends—that's discussion.

You are a constant participant in discussions and conferences.

Perhaps your failure to recognize this before has prevented you from taking part in activities you consider quite important.

For instance, have you failed to join in discussion at Parent-Teacher Association meetings?

Do you sit mutely by at office conferences?

Do you fail to do your duty as a citizen by not even going to political meetings because you feel you could not join in the discussion?

How much have *you* lost by such failures on your part?

How much have *others* failed to gain because you sat mum, perhaps holding back an idea or ideas that could have solved major problems—all because you felt you could not participate in the discussion at hand?

THE DAILY CONFERENCE:
A SUCCESSFUL CONTEST _____

You take part in such discussions and/or conferences every day. It may only be a chance meeting at the water cooler or while waiting for the elevator. It may be an interruption that calls you out of a big meeting for a brief exchange in the hall.

No matter where it is, how it comes about, what it concerns—remember that it is a contest. It is the moment in a day when you can succeed or fail.

What makes success?

Your memory! Your memory is the weapon that helps you win the contest.

What good is a sales idea, for instance, if you don't have facts and figures to back up the scheme?

How can you convince your boss to make a certain investment, if you appear to be "talking through your hat" without seeming basis in fact?

How can you get your school board to make the progressive move you envision if you fail to convince its members with the use of facts and figures?

How can you clinch a simple sale without knowing your product and its qualities and being able to answer the questions your prospect may toss at you?

A hundred possibilities might pass you by every day—if you aren't aware that you are engaged in a continuing contest. And the "playing field" of that contest is the discussion and the conference.

What, then, should you do? How can you be prepared for any exigency that may arise?

KNOW YOUR FACTS _____

We come right back, now, to the basic premise. You have to be well armed with *facts.*

You can't demand the best without them. You are much in the position of the young man who, being interviewed for a new job, demanded a high salary despite the fact he had no experience in that line of work.

Asked about why he felt he deserved so much money, he replied:

"Well, it's so much harder work when you don't know anything about it."

It's much harder when you aren't prepared.

As soon as possible, when you know you are going to participate in any form of discussion or conference, start to prepare.

Research the subject, if you don't already have a working knowledge of it. Read as much as you can about what is to be talked about—and absorb it thoroughly.

If you are familiar with the subject matter, refresh your memory by going over the pertinent details.

Whether you've had to start from scratch or are just refreshing your recollection, try to piece together the important facts into an easily rememberable pattern.

As I pointed out a few moments ago, there are several ways in which this can be done.

Let us look at a few of them and see how they can be utilized to forearm you well.

THE MENTAL HOOK LIST

As an example of what you might encounter, let us assume you are going into a P.T.A. meeting to attempt to get hot lunch service arranged at the school your children attend.

You prepare your argument after having studied the situation at other schools. You discovered, let us say, that:

> 1. *A majority of the children benefit by being able to eat their lunch in a more leisurely fashion. They don't have to rush home, gobble a meal, and rush back to make the afternoon session.*
> 2. *The children get an opportunity of associating out of class regimentation and under conditions that stimulate social intercourse of a sort they will encounter later in life.*
> 3. *A sense of responsibility is created because each child has a task to perform in the serving of the meals and the setting and clearing of the tables.*
> 4. *As an alternative to sandwiches that are brought by the children who live too far to go home, the hot lunch is far preferable dietetically.*
> 5. *For children of many families, the hot lunch, properly balanced, provides the basic planned diet for the day.*

6. In many cases, parents spend too little time in preparing a child's lunch, so that the school lunch would be preferable.

Now, to keep these points in mind, let us utilize the Mental Hook List.

This is what the six-point argument would look like:

*1. Me—picture yourself as parent to a horde of children, so may that there isn't enough room at the table to feed them all at one time. Therefore each child **hurriedly eats** while you rush back and forth serving them.*
*2. Shoe—picture a well-trained army going through its drill patterns, every soldier neatly dressed but the **regimentation is broken** by the fact that none is wearing shoes.*
*3. Kitten—picture a litter of kittens who would rather gaily play all day, but instead are made to **set tables** with saucers of milk and then **clear away** the empty saucers.*
*4. Table—picture a buffet table overloaded with **sandwiches** that keep slipping off onto the floor.*
*5. Finger—picture yourself having to **plan a diet** and, knowing that there are five basic ingredients, you count them on the fingers of your hand to see you have them all.*
*6. Sticks—picture yourself in **too much of a hurry** to make a meal and so you go out into the garden and pick twigs and sticks and toss them onto a plate and serve it as a salad.*

USING A CHAIN OF THOUGHT

We can use the same example of the P.T.A. meeting to see how a chain of connected thoughts would help in remembering your arguments in favor of hot lunches.

Going back to the six points you wish to make in your presentation to the group, let us find a word that would symbolize each.

The first point might be represented by *hurry.*

The second point by *regiment.*

The third by *responsible.*

The fourth by *sandwich.*

The fifth by *plan.*

The sixth by *time.*

By readjusting the words in the following fashion, here is one chain of thought you might construct:

Regiment

> *A regiment that is responsible*

Responsible

> *for a plan*

Plan

> *to supply sandwiches*

Sandwich

> *is hurrying*

Hurry

> *to be on time.*

Time

By picturing the thought that you have created in your chain at the right, you can recall the key words in the left hand column and the six points of your presentation are clearly in your mind.

DON'T GET FLUSTERED _____

Having the facts at your finger-tips, you have armed yourself well. But now comes a second important prerequisite in the contest.

You must not allow anything to throw you off stride.

Do you find that if anyone asks a question of you, you suddenly find your mind going blank?

You will remember that early in this book I mentioned that people often asked me if under the pressure of questioning on the $64,000 Question I didn't find that I could not remember the answer. As I pointed out, you will not forget if you know the answer.

The same thing applies here.

If you know your facts, no one is going to be able to "throw" you. If you are sure of your ground, no amount of questioning is going to make you forget the facts.

Thus well armed and knowing that no one is going to be able to fluster you, you can plow headstrong into the contest. Your opponents in the discussion or conference need not be feared. The means to success are on your side.

"It's easy to say 'don't get flustered, but what do you do if you do become flustered?" you may ask.

The first rule of combatting such a situation is to regain your calm. Instead of tensing and beginning to worry, smile! You will be surprised how a smile will relax you. And once relaxed, you get back onto your train of thought.

One story of keeping calm concerns the days when plays were done live on the radio. An actor was playing the part of De Lawd in Marc Connelly's *Green Pastures* when a fellow actor forgot his lines and froze.

The first actor reassuringly came to the rescue by just remaining calm and thinking coolly.

"Son," he said, "you is nervous before me and I can understand that. But I is de Lord, and I knows what is on your mind." Whereupon he supplied the missing lines.

BE SURE OF YOUR FACTS

In assembling facts, one of the most important steps you must take is evaluating the material you have assembled.

It is simply not enough to collect information. You must be able to judge its worth. Your ability to classify and test facts will not only prove useful in preparing your own material, it will also be of great help to you in judging the arguments of those against whom you are pitted in the contests of discussion and conferences.

Facts are of three kinds—demonstrable, historical and statistical. The first type comprises those which you experience yourself. Your five senses play the major role in this gathering of fact. But it is not always possible for you to experience all things, so you collect many of these demonstrable facts from others. They are, however, things that under different circumstances you would have experienced yourself.

You often get such facts from newspapers, magazines, or books. They may come from a television or radio program. For instance, in *PBB: An American Tragedy,* by Edwin Chen, you can read that the United States Congress banned the manufacture of PCBs as of January 1, 1979.[1]

This is information you could have obtained first hand, had you been in Washington at the time. But since you probably were not, you have to rely on the book to transmit this to you. So you see that although most demonstrable facts that you use in discussion come from other sources, it might have been possible to have obtained them first hand.

Historical facts are those that, of course, you could not have possibly verified by experience. They relate to events that took place in the distant past. They are accepted largely on the basis of records by which they can be identified.

OTHER FACTS

In this way we accept the facts presented in history books. We accept the word of authors that their material has been verified by documents, letters, and other records.

So that when you read in *A History of Civilization,* by Brinton, Christopher, and Wolff, that Socrates, a stone-mason by trade, wrote no books and held no formal teaching post but was one of the greatest teachers in human history,[2] you accept it as fully as though you would be able to verify it yourself.

As far as historical facts go, you always have to rely on such sources for your information.

Statistics, in actuality, are a special kind of facts much like demonstrable ones. They could be verified by you, if you had the time to do so. But since this is usually impossible, you accept them just as you do other demonstrable—and historical—facts.

Of course, in statistics, as in history, you have to be careful of your source. Statistics are frequently used in presenting arguments in discussions and conferences. They are the foundation for much thought and for many decisions.

---

[1] Copyright © 1979 by Edwin Chen. Published by Prentice-Hall, Inc., Englewood Cliffs, New Jersey 07632.

[2] Copyright © 1976 by Prentice-Hall, Inc., Englewood Cliffs, New Jersey 07632.

TESTING FACTS _____

Since statistics and other facts should be taken from sound sources, it is a good idea to know how you can "test" facts before using them. There are four tests that you should make:

> 1. **What is the source?** *Make as sure as you can that your source is a reliable one. This is especially true in the case of statistics. Remember, figures can be made to "lie" and you don't want to use statistics that have been twisted to suit someone else's purposes.*
>
> 2. **Are they reasonable?** *Facts should appear to be reasonable according to your own standards. For example, if you were told that the earth was recently proved to be flat, you would not accept this as it is not in accord with the knowledge you have of the earth in relationship to the rest of the universe.*
>
> 3. **Do they agree with other facts?** *If facts disagree with another set of facts you would naturally be suspicious of both sets. If they agree, however, you are safe in accepting them as valid.*
>
> 4. **Are they acceptable to others?** *This need not have anything to do with the ultimate reliability of the facts, but having your facts acceptable to others makes them more valid for use. It is pointless using facts that will not be accepted.*

Having selected your facts, and tested them, you now are ready to keep them at your finger tips.

Use whatever method you prefer to make the facts vivid in your memory. With a clear picture in your mind of the facts you need to present for your side of the case, and with sound facts to prove your point, the discussion or the conference is yours to win.

16

HOW TO REMEMBER NAMES AND FACES

I cannot tell what the dickens his name is.
Shakespeare, *The Merry Wives of Windsor.*

The inability to remember names and faces is an annoying thing—both for you and for the person not remembered. As I pointed out many times in the chapters preceding, it will profit you many times over to improve your memory for people's names.

People whom you fail to recognize by sight, or by name, can assume only one thing: that you have no interest in them. It is to your best advantage to be able to place the face *and* the name.

The purpose of this chapter is to help you if you have a problem of recalling names and tying them together with faces.

On the following four pages are the pictures of sixteen persons.

I would like to introduce them to you one by one:

This is
JEAN MC BRIDE

This is
FRANK SHILLER

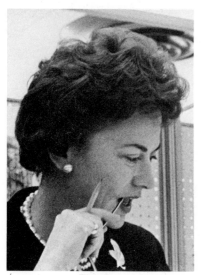

This is
EDWINA CAREY

This is
LEONARD LAMBERT

This is
ROSE PALAZZO

This is
SPENCER NOLDISH

This is
MARY CONNELLY

This is
SAUL SOWETSKI

This is
PAT HOPPER

This is
HELEN HARDY

This is
JOE WEISS

This is
DAVID MACHOVER

This is
ABIGAIL SINGER

This is
MARTHA RUHLING

This is
PERCY MANNIKER

This is
ERNEST JUDD

Well now, you have just met sixteen charming people. They are average, everyday persons just like the ones you might meet anywhere else at some other time. It is a sort of mixed group, some older and some younger, but in general it is an average group.

How many of the sixteen persons you just met, then, do you think you can remember?

Well, here are a few of them. Why not write their names under their pictures right now—without turning back to check.

Did you do all right?

Well, let's see. The two persons on top (from left to right) are: Edwina Carey and Rose Palazzo.

In the same order, the bottom two are Spencer Noldish and Jean McBride.

Here are a few more of the people you just met. How many of this group do you remember?

If your memory for names and faces was working perfectly you would have spotted Joe Weiss and Frank Shiller on the top and Mary Connelly and Saul Sowetski on the bottom.

HOW TO REMEMBER THESE PEOPLE

Well, you have just met a group of sixteen persons. You probably remembered some of their names. But you should have been able to recall all sixteen names the first time through. If you successfully applied the lessons you learned in the earlier chapters, perhaps you did remember them all.

In any event, let us go back over the names and see if you can devise a way in which each name will become a meaningful thing in your memory.

Let's look back at Jean McBride. Remember all the songs that have been written about girls named Jean? There was Jeannie with the Light Brown Hair and My Bonnie Jeannie. It seems that pretty girls named Jean have often inspired the poetic talents of men. This Jean McBride (she, like Bonnie Jeannie, is Scottish, as her name tells you) is also a *bonnie* girl. Lovely enough to be a *bride.* And so this lovely girl who looks like a bride should not cause too much trouble in remembering the name of Jean McBride.

Now here is Frank Shiller. Did you notice his sincere, open, truthful-looking face? This young man is not one to be deceitful. He looks as though he'd tell the truth, no matter how much it may hurt—because the truth means much to such a *frank* person. His serious demeanor reminds you of a student, doesn't it? He looks quite studious and probably is a keen student of everything he does. A student is a *scholar* and that is pretty close to Shiller. So this *truthful student* is Frank Shiller.

Edwina Carey is a handsome woman, is she not? She looks quite successful and much as though she might be a career woman. The cut of her face is a little away from the feminine; a little like a man's face. Her name Edwina is the feminine version of the man's name Edwin. And she's obviously successful—a *winner.* So Edwina should not be hard to remember. Her appearance of being a *career* woman will help with her last name. Career-Carey. This is a successful business woman, *a winner* in her *career*—Edwina Carey.

Here's Leonard Lambert again. Of course, his names both begin with the letter "L" and so that's a big help right away. Did you notice the strong lion-like face he has? It is called *leonine* and you can remember that Leo the Lion is Leonard. In contrast, the white tufts of hair on his temples and the woolly mustache are a lot like a *lamb*. Lamb for Lambert; and you have the legend of the *Lion and the Lamb* all rolled up in Mr. Leonard Lambert.

The charming woman who smiles at you knowingly is Rose Palazzo. She is wonderfully well preserved for her age, don't you think? It is as though she still is at the height of her bloom. And, with that sharp twinkle in her eye, undoubtedly she still is in bloom—a late-blooming *rose* that graces the garden. Her friendly look makes you sure she'd be a *pal* to you and that will help you remember that your pal is named Palazzo. Also you can recall that Palazzo means *palace* in Italian and there is a regal look in Rose Palazzo's face. Royalty always lives in a palace. So that lovely blooming *rose* in the *palace* garden is your newly acquired *friend*, Rose Palazzo.

Spencer Noldish is a neat dresser. Look at how carefully his hair is combed, his tie is neatly tied, his shirt collar is uncrushed and his jacket hangs just right. In fact he is so careful about his clothes, he probably wears *suspenders* to keep his trousers hanging just so. Spencer wears suspenders; and he's not such an old man despite the wise look he has. Oh, he's not young, but he's *not so oldish*—and that should make it easy for you to recall the name of the *not so oldish* man who is so neat he must wear *suspenders*—Spencer Noldish.

Isn't Mary Connelly pretty? Such a happy face and that lovely smile that never leaves her mouth! Obviously quite a *merry* girl, is Mary. The curly hair she has seems to be quite natural; and *curly* isn't so far from Connelly, is it? Also you might notice that she has a college girl look about her—perhaps this *merry* girl went to *Cornell!* In any case, she's Mary Connelly and she's quite easy to remember.

Saul Sowetski is another person with a happy disposition. He seems to exude well-being from his face. It shines just like the sun. And the *sun* is well known as *Sol,* so that Mr. Sowetski's first name is a natural. Did you notice, too, the sweet kindliness that shines through the face of this sun? Yes, *sweet* is the word for Mr. Sowetski. If you think he looks like the outdoor type who loves to go skiing, let's all go along; and if we were with Saul Sowetski on a *sunny* day, *so we'd ski,* wouldn't we?

Here's an intelligent looking young lady. Yes, Pat Hopper looks as though she has everything down just *pat.* She knows what she's about. And you may have noticed that she has her hair *patted* neatly down, too. Doesn't she look quite young? You'd think she was just out of the *hop*-scotch stage! Well, this *happy* young *hopper* has a *pat* way of helping you recall that she's Pat Hopper.

There was once a lady whose face, it was said, had launched a thousand ships. Don't you think that this Helen is just as beautiful a lady as that Helen of antiquity? Of course, Helen Hardy is an alliteration and *H-H* will help you remember her. But if you think of *Helen of Troy* and remember that it was many years ago that she lived, you might also think that many years ago this girl's ancestors were probably *pioneers* in the wide open spaces of this country's West. That wide-open face and forehead will recall those vast plains and the *hardy* folks who pioneered them. Her determined jaw is a sure sign that she can be a *hard* person to try to fool or be non-sensical with. But she's a beautiful Helen and she's sure to be a Hardy one.

Well, Joe Weiss is a *jovial* fellow, isn't he? It seems as though he's always got a *joke* on the tip of his tongue that's just going to convulse you and everyone in the group. Oh, he's a *joker* all right, but there's no denying that he is a pretty clever fellow. In fact, he has a very *wise* look to his face. His *white* hair is a clue, too, to the fact that his name, Weiss, means white in German. This *wise* old *joker* is Joe Weiss, and you can't miss him.

Young David Machover is ready to go out and challenge the world. He's a recent college graduate and he's got the fire of his namesake who didn't even fear Goliath. Yes, Mr. Machover is a *David* who will tackle the biggest things in life and overcome them. In fact, he could well *make over* not only his own life—in its change from student days to the more serious aspects of the business world—but he might well *make* some Goliaths take *cover* if they stand in the way of his progress. David Machover has far to go.

"None sings so sweet as the nightingale," goes a line of poetry, and it is true that when it comes to *singers* it is hard to beat that little bird called the *nightingale*. So that Abigail Singer should present no problems to you in remembering her name. Did you notice that she has an appearance of gusto; she seems ready to burst into song at a moment's notice. And she wears her hair in wing-like fashion over her ears, just as though she were a bird. The *nightingale singer* is our Abigail Singer.

This motherly person with the kindly face and white hair is Martha Ruhling. Isn't it a lovely old-fashioned name, Martha, and doesn't it go with a motherly person? In fact, she looks like she might be a *mother,* or *"ma"* to her children, which makes it comparatively easy to remember that her name is Martha. Being a mother, of course, makes her the "boss" of the house—a virtual *ruler.* She probably is a *mother* who *rules* her home very well, this Martha Ruhling.

Percy Manniker is a clean-cut young man who looks as though he might be an actor, or perhaps a model. Did you notice how he holds his lips, sort of *pursed,* so that you should always remember his name is Percy? As for being a model, if you think of him as a *mannequin* with *pursed* lips you'll have no difficulty with Percy Manniker.

That is such a sincere-looking face that Ernest Judd has! He certainly is a straightforward person, as *earnest* as you can find a man. And his intelligent face, with lovely white hair, and kindly, understanding eyes, makes you feel sure that he could be a *judge.* Certainly you wouldn't want to appear—if you had to—before a more *earnest* looking *judge* than a man like Ernest Judd, would you?

FITTING FACES TO NAMES

You've been through the whole group, now. Thus armed, you should have no difficulty in looking at any one of the faces in this group and coming up with the name.

However, there sometimes is another problem you may encounter. Can you fit the faces to the names, if necessary? In other words, can you accomplish the reverse of fitting names to the right faces?

It might well be, for instance, that you are at a cocktail party and have just been introduced to everyone there, when the host asks you, as a favor, to please ask Ms. Ruhling what she wants to drink.

Sure, you recall having met a Ms. Ruhling—what was her name? Oh yes, Martha Ruhling—but which one of the women standing in the other room is she?

Or perhaps, someone has said to you that Mr. Lambert would make a good prospect for you, because he's in the market for just the product you are selling. As a matter of fact, you might even broach the subject now so that you can arrange for an appointment at his office later in the week.

Wonderful, you think, I'll walk right over to Mr. Lambert this minute and wait for an opening in the conversation that I can utilize. But which of those four men standing in the corner, laughing so heartily, is Leonard Lambert?

Well, this can be a problem, but it can be solved by the same method as you have solved the matching names to faces problem. Just think of the name, recall your associations, and find the face to fit those clues.

For instance, there are twelve pictures down the opposite side of this page. Each has a number under it. Try matching the right number to the list of names that follows:

ERNEST JUDD   _____
MARTHA RUHLING   _____
HELEN HARDY   _____
SPENCER NOLDISH   _____
LEONARD LAMBERT   _____
PAT HOPPER   _____
DAVID MACHOVER   _____
JEAN McBRIDE   _____

Were you able to match the names to the faces correctly? These are the numbers you should have written down against the names on the previous page:

ERNEST JUDD	1	LEONARD LAMBERT	8
MARTHA RUHLING	2	PAT HOPPER	6
HELEN HARDY	7	DAVID MACHOVER	12
SPENCER NOLDISH	4	JEAN McBRIDE	9

GENERAL RULES FOR REMEMBERING NAMES _____

Now that you have learned how to join names and faces together, a further step that is important in the task of remembering names and faces is that of remembering names over a long period of time.

By seeing the face and hearing the name at the same time, and by working out an association to help you recall the name and tie it to the face, you have a simple key to your immediate problem. But what do you do to recall a name six months or six years later? Do you react like the professor I once knew who tried desperately to pin down the names of hundreds of former students at a reunion. He was greeting as many former students as he could remember, when suddenly he saw a very familiar face approach. He rushed over, failed to place the name, and so said:

"What are you doing now?"

"Well," said the familiar face, "this semester I'm in your 10 o'clock class."

To make sure that names will stick with you and return to mind when you need them in years to come, follow these simple rules:

1. Make sure you have heard the name clearly.

2. Repeat the name, in conversation, as soon as possible after you have been introduced.

3. Use the name at least once again—or if you can, more often—in the ensuing conversation.

4. Look for some association that you can link to the name.

5. Repeat the name several times as soon as you have a chance.

6. Later at the first opportunity, write the name on a piece of paper.

Some names will provide you with associations very simply. There are names of places, such as France, London, Rome, Poland. There are names of animals, such as Lamb, Byrd, Lyon, Wolfe. There are names like occupations, such as Cooper, Smith, Taylor, Carpenter, Mason. There are names of metals and minerals, such as Stone, Gold, Silver. There are names like adjectives, such as Rich, Long, Green, White. There are names of famous persons, such as Lincoln, Franklin, Webster, O'Neill, Barrymore.

Others will require a little work to get your association keyed in quickly. But with a little practice, you will find that these associations will come more and more readily.

A FINAL RUN THROUGH

The sixteen people we met earlier in this chapter, and again as we went along learning how to remember names and faces, should pose little problem to you now. Here are some of those faces again. Why don't you write the names, as you recall them, under each face.

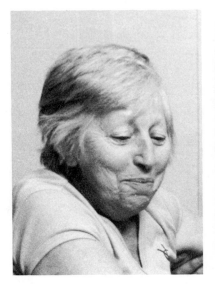

17

IMPROVE YOUR READING

The true art of memory is the art of attention.
Samuel Johnson, *The Idler.*

Thomas Carlyle once said that all one can do to educate people is to teach them to read, after which they can educate themselves.

This is doubtless an exaggeration. But there is no doubt that anyone who can do a good job of reading has available a tool that will serve well throughout life.

Does it seem strange to you to see the phrase "a good job of reading"? Certainly, you probably think, anyone who buys a book can read. True—to an extent. But how well do *you* read?

Most people today can pick up books, magazines, or newspapers and read them. That is the result of the widespread education we have in this age. But whether they read easily or not, and whether they comprehend what the writer is saying, is another matter.

Too often, neither is the case.

HOW THE EYE TRAVELS

Tests have shown that everyone reads in a somewhat jerky fashion.
Some   people's   eyes   jump   from   word   to word   and   they   are   considerably   slowed   down   as they   read.

Reading in such a fashion is a waste of physical energy and a taker of valuable time.

Other people   manage to   read a sentence   in groups of   two or three   words at a   time and thus save a little   in both energy and time.

Some   people   can   not   do better   than   read   a   word   at   a time   and   then   only   by   seeing each   letter   separately   and virtually   spelling   every- thing   as   they   go   along.

They read. But at any one of the three speeds demonstrated, how much do you think they absorb and understand? How much can be retained for better usage of the power of memory? How can memory-efficiency be achieved with a slow-down of reading such as that?

In addition, most people fail to distinguish between es- sential ideas and illustrative material. They fail to grasp the relation- ship between main and subordinate points. They fail—even when numbering, lettering, captioning, or paragraphing is used—to note the writer's sequence of thought.

Scores of investigations have borne out these facts.

So it is important then for you to ask yourself how well you are able to read and whether you should not attempt to improve your reading ability.

Of course, I don't think of any one of you as being as incap- able of comprehension as the woman whose friend got tired of always getting new dates for her. It seemed this woman was quiet and reserved and her vivacious friend finally suggested one day:

"I don't mind digging up dates for us, but you just sit around like a zombie and never open your mouth. Why don't you read up on something to talk about?"

The woman said she would try. On their next date, when one of those painful silences developed, this woman gulped once or twice and then tried to do her share:

"Isn't it too bad," she said, "what happened to Marie Antoinette?"

READ TO UNDERSTAND

But it is essential, if you want to improve your reading, that you *read to understand.* Understanding in this case requires remembering, too. Otherwise you may find yourself in a situation much like that told of Gabriel Pascal, the late motion picture magnate. It seemed he wanted the screen rights to a minor play by George Bernard Shaw and Shaw wired him that he wanted $8,000 for the rights.

"I'll give you $4,000," was Pascal's wired reply.

"You must have misunderstood my original demand," protested Shaw in a collect telegram. "I asked for $80,000, not $8,000." Pascal promptly replied: "Excuse error. I'll give you $40,000."

E. L. Thorndike, the famous psychologist who did much experimental work in reading habits and abilities, once said that "reading is reasoning."

In other words when you read properly you are not only transferring automatically what your eyes see to your brain. If you read well, you are interpreting, questioning, comprehending, criticizing, comparing: it is a whole process of thought and remembering.

AN AMUSING TEST RESULT

Thorndike showed astonishingly—and amusingly—how little of what they read people absorbed. He had a group of people read the following sentence:

Nearly fifteen thousand of the city's workers joined the parade on September seventh, and passed before two hundred thousand cheering spectators. There were workers of both sexes in the parade, though the men far outnumbered the women.

Don't look back at that passage. Get a pencil and answer these questions:

What was said about the number of persons who joined in the parade? _____

Which sex was in the majority? _____

What did the people who looked at the parade do as it passed? _____

How many people were there altogether? _____

Where were the workers from? _____

How did you do on the answers? They should read: *They marched past the spectators; Men; They cheered; Nearly two hundred and fifteen thousand; The city.*

It only required a little understanding of what you read to get the correct answers. But Thorndike found that his subjects answered such things as:

"They joined" for the first question;

"Both in parade" for the second;

"Two hundred thousand cheering spectators" for the third;

A variety of figures for the fourth; and

"They were workers of the seventh," for the fifth.

Although some of the answers were true, they did not answer what was asked and in the case of the answer for the fifth question, it seems the subject was confused between the parading people and the date.

It is necessary, then, to understand what you read. You must select the correct elements of a sentence, a paragraph, or a chapter. You must read with more than your eyes—you must also read with your brain.

I am acquainted with a newspaper reporter, a man trained in the use of words and meaning, who committed a gross error when he quoted a written statement as its complete opposite. It seems, he later discovered, that he failed to see the word "not" in the sentence.

These things can happen to you. They must not, however, if you are to read properly and if you are to increase the power of remembering successfully.

SOME WAYS TO IMPROVE

How, then, can your reading be improved?

The first thing to be done in reading is to get an over-all picture—a *Bird's-Eye View*—as you learned to do in Chapter 9, "A BIRD'S-EYE VIEW."

Map out a general idea of how the piece you are reading is laid out. Your first step in bettering your reading ability is to discover what is contained in the item or book you are reading.

Look especially for summation paragraphs. In an article these should appear at the end; in a book they may appear at the end of every chapter. Even if there are no formal summations, the closing paragraphs usually are written in such a manner as to summarize. These help you materially in grasping what the author has in mind.

The second important step is recognizing the essential elements of the article or book. Having gone over the general ground, you now are to look for places to dig so that you can strike gold. When you come across "gold ore," underline it. Underlining as you read puts at your fingertips the most valuable ideas. Marking key passages that will be important to you will save precious time when you review.

You should also adopt the habit of making marginal notes. Always read with a pencil in hand. Write your ideas, comments and reactions in the margin while they are fresh in your mind. A note made when the thought strikes you preserves today's idea for future use.

The final step of economical reading is the careful studying of the detail. Details are always best handled after the over-all structure is established in your mind. In that way the framework can be filled in solidly.

WHAT ABOUT READING SPEED?

One of the greatest problems of waste in reading is that of speed. Too often people read too slowly to read effectively. It is essential to try to increase your reading speed so that there is less interference with the process of remembering.

The more effort reading requires, the less energy will remain for acquiring a memory of what you read.

As I pointed out at the start of this chapter, most people read either in small groups of words, thus having the eye jerk along like a beginner learning to use an automobile with standard transmission, on an almost letter-by-letter basis as if spelling the words out.

The most efficient way to read is to grasp the words in larger groups on every line.

At first it would   be advisable to try   to read lines
in three movements   of the eye so that   there is less jerky
action taken by   the eye muscles.   If you find that
this method comes   to you with ease   then try next to
increase the amount that the eye   takes in at a time by
dividing the line automatically   into two sections and only
having a single jump on every   line to accomplish in two
movements what it took three   to accomplish before.

The faster you learn to read, the more words you are going to grasp at one time—and therefore the easier it will be for you to remember what you read. By reading in large chunks, instead of piecemeal, you are making meaningful "wholes" out of your reading matter. These meaningful "wholes" are vastly superior to the arbitrarily broken-up phrases of slipshod reading.

ENCOURAGE YOURSELF BY PRACTICE _____

One of the best ways to encourage and increase speed in reading is to practice. Get from magazines—probably the digest-sized ones are best for this—a number of articles each of less than one thousand words. Hold a clock to yourself as you read each for the first time and mark down the exact time it took to read the piece.

Set aside a fifteen-minute period each day for six weeks and read several of these pieces every day, each week timing yourself again for each of the pieces.

You will find that you might be reading at an average of about three hundred and fifty words a minute at the start. By the end of a week your speed should have increased by as much as one hundred per cent. And by the end of the six-week period, you will be amazed at how much more rapidly you will be able to read these pieces—and everything.

The practice of reading pieces you know and understand helps your eye adjust to the idea of accommodating half a line—or in the case of a newspaper column, a whole line—at a time.

With greater speed and with increased understanding of how to get the most out of your reading, the task of further increasing your power to remember will become a simple one.

You will be able to laugh at William James, for you will be using not ten per cent but one hundred per cent of your memory power.

You will be able to use your memory-efficiency to its fullest capacity.

You will find life holding open new vistas to you—all because of your power to remember.

You will be able to class yourself with the businessperson who one day met a man and said:

"Well, if it isn't Paul Millar, the salesperson I met up in Vermont one rainy night eight years ago at the Montpelier railway station."

The salesperson turned on his heel and said, "Goodbye."

"Just a minute, Paul," said the businessperson, "aren't you going to try to sell me something?"

"No," the salesperson replied. "I sell memory courses now."

Remember! And success if yours.

Remember! And happiness is yours.

Remember! And the power to accomplish becomes a power beyond belief!

REMEMBER!

INDEX